Illustrator:
Howard Chaney

Editor:
Walter Kelly, M.A.

Editor in Chief:
Sharon Coan, M.S. Ed.

Creative Director:
Elayne Roberts

Associate Designer:
Denise Bauer

Cover Art:
Denise Bauer

Imaging:
Alfred Lau
Ralph Olmedo, Jr.

Product Manager:
Phil Garcia

Publishers:
Rachelle Cracchiolo, M.S. Ed.
Mary Dupuy Smith, M.S. Ed.

Primary

Written by Ruth M. Young, M.S. Ed.

Teacher Created Materials, Inc.
P.O. Box 1040
Huntington Beach, CA 92647
©1997 Teacher Created Materials, Inc.
Made in the U. S. A.
ISBN-1-57690-381-8

The classroom teacher may reproduce copies of materials in this book for classroom use only. The reproduction of any part for an entire school or school system is strictly prohibited. No part of this publication may be transmitted, stored, or recorded in any form without written permission from the publisher.

Table of Contents

Introduction 3

Comparing Earth and Mars

How Big Is Mars? 4

Where Is Mars? 6

Martian Motion 8

Race of the Planets 9

Phases of Earth's Moon 14

Martian Moons 18

How's the Weather Up There? 21

Mars Pathfinder Mission

Build Your Own Microrover 31

Slower Than a Speeding Snail 36

Design a Robot 38

3-D View of Mars 41

Incoming Command 43

The Little Rover That Could 49

The Martians Have Landed!

Launching to Mars 63

Off to Mars (assessment project) 66

Postscript from Mars 76

Resources (annotated)

Related Books and Periodicals 77

Related Materials 78

Web Sites 79

CD-ROMs 80

#2381 Exploring Mars　　　　　　　　　　　*© Teacher Created Materials, Inc.*

Introduction

Earth

Mars

Mars has fascinated people ever since they began to watch the night sky. The first astronomers noticed that all the stars remained in fixed positions, except for five* which appeared to wander the sky. They called these *planets*, which means "wanderer." The red planet reminded them of bloody battlefields and was named Mars, for the Roman god of war. Earth's astronomical symbol shows crossed lines representing the equator and axis. Mars' symbol represents the shield and spear of the Roman god.

In 1877 the Italian astronomer Giovanni Schiaparelli observed Mars through a telescope and reported seeing *canali* crisscrossing the bright areas of the planets. *Canali* is Italian for channels or grooves but was translated into English as *canal*, which led some people to think intelligent life existed on Mars. In 1897 H.G. Wells wrote *The War of the Worlds* about Martians invading Earth. Three years later, Percival Lowell, a wealthy Bostonian amateur astronomer, built the Lowell Observatory in Flagstaff, Arizona. Lowell devoted his time to the study of Mars, making drawings of the polar ice caps and an intricate network of lines which he thought were the canals bringing water from the ice to the warmer regions near the equator. In 1971 photographs relayed back to Earth from the unmanned *Mariner 9* satellite in orbit 1,000 miles (1,600 km) above Mars showed areas which had once been flooded with water but were now dry. No canals were seen, but extensive dust storms were raging all across the planet.

Our fascination with Mars increased with the *Mariner* information. The United States initiated the *Viking* missions in 1976, landing two unmanned spacecraft using maps created with the data from *Mariner 9*. *Viking 1* had been scheduled to land on Mars on July 4, 1976, the 200th anniversary of our nation. A suitable landing site was not found by that date, so the landing took place on July 20th, seven years after the first landing on the moon. The identical *Viking* landers were mini-science laboratories that supplied scientists on Earth with incredible information about Mars but found no life forms.

The Mars *Pathfinder* was launched from Earth on December 4, 1996, landing on Mars on July 4, 1997. This time there was a microrover on board the landing craft. No larger than a small microwave oven, it roamed the area near the lander, testing rocks and soil, and taking photographs of the area, which was just 525 miles southeast of the *Viking 1* landing site. Data including weather information and images of the landscape were relayed back to the Jet Propulsion Laboratory in Pasadena, California, where scientists downloaded it and continue to report the exciting results to the world.

Among today's students are the future Martians. As early as 2011, they may be part of a crew sent from Earth to be the first humans on Mars. The data received from unmanned satellites and landers on Mars will help pave the way for these early explorers. The late Dr. Carl Sagan, famed astronomer, predicted that someday Mars would be made habitable and "The Martians will be us."

* Uranus, Neptune, and Pluto were not discovered until better telescopes were developed.

Comparing Earth and Mars

How Big Is Mars?

Overview

Students will learn the relative sizes of the nine planets in our solar system by making paper scale models of them.

Background

The nine planets in our solar system vary in size from Jupiter, the largest at 11 times the diameter of Earth, to Pluto, smaller than Earth's moon. The chart below gives the information required to make scale models of the planets in our solar system.

Planet Diameters									
Categories	Mercury	Venus	Earth	Mars	Jupiter	Saturn	Uranus	Neptune	Pluto
Diameter in Miles (Kilometers)	3,050 (4,880)	7,563 (12,100)	7,973 (12,756)	4,246 (6,794)	89,365 (142,984)	75,335 (120,536)	31,938 (51,100)	30,938 (49,500)	1,438 (2,300)
Diameter Relative to Earth's	.38	.95	1.0	.53	11.2	9.4	4	3.9	.18
* Radius of Scale Model	2 cm	4.8 cm	5 cm	2.5 cm	55 cm	47 cm	20 cm	19.5 cm	1 cm
Suggested Color	gray	white	blue	red	orange	yellow	green	blue	black

*The scale for this model of the planets is based upon the radius of Earth being 5 cm. Metric measurements are used to simplify drawing the scale model.

Materials

- four colors of butcher paper for the largest planets
- five different colors of construction paper for the remaining planets
- string
- nine file cards
- pencil compass for drawing circles
- meter stick
- **Optional**: colored pictures of the planets taken by satellites

Request Solar System Lithograph Set EP-339 8/95 from NASA, Education Division, Mail Code FE, Washington DC 20546-0001. Set includes the sun, nine planets, and Earth's moon.

Preparation

Note: *This scale model of the planets may be done by the teacher or students, depending upon their ability levels. The directions are to be used if the students are constructing the models. If the teacher is going to make them, file cards for the smaller planets will not be needed.*

Make a file card for each of the planets, recording its name, actual diameter, and the radius being used for this model. Draw a line the length of the radius on the cards for the five smaller planets (Mercury, Venus, Earth, Mars, and Pluto). This will enable students to set their pencil compasses to the correct radius before drawing the circles for the model.

#2381 Exploring Mars 4 © *Teacher Created Materials, Inc.*

How Big Is Mars? *(cont.)*

Preparation *(cont.)*

Cut pieces of string the lengths of the radius of the largest planets plus about four inches (10 cm). Punch a hole in the middle of one long edge of each planet's card and tie the corresponding string to it. Tie a loop in the end of the string so a pencil can be placed in it. When the string is stretched to its full length, it should equal the radius needed for this model.

Pin the colored paper to a bulletin board or place it on the floor. Center the index card at the top of the long edge or center of the paper and hold it so it will not move. Place the pencil in the loop and stretch the string. Draw a semicircle arc for Jupiter and Saturn.

When drawing Neptune or Uranus, place the card in the center of the paper and tack or hold it in place. Stretch the string with the pencil and draw a large circle.

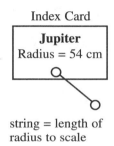
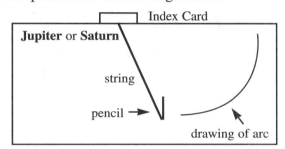
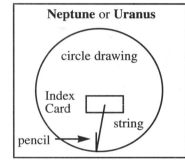

Cut out the planet and then label it with its name and diameter in miles and kilometers. Tape the planets together so they can be compared, superimposing them as shown in the drawing below.

For Discussion

- Have students compare the sizes of the planets, beginning with Earth and Jupiter. Fold the model of the Earth in half (to show its diameter) and let students guess how many "Earths" would fit across Jupiter. Count the number by moving the model Earth across Jupiter (*11*).

- Compare the size of Mars and the Earth by folding Mars in half and having students guess how many times the planet would fit across Earth (*about 2*).

Follow Up

- Make a model of Earth's moon, using this same scale. The radius would be 1.4 cm. Compare this scale model with those of Earth and Mars.

- The sun is a star with the diameter of 870,000 miles (1,392,000 km). On this scale its diameter would be 10.9 meters. Make a string this length and stretch it from the edge of Jupiter to its full length to compare the diameter of the sun to the planets.

Comparing Earth and Mars

Where Is Mars?

Overview

A scale model of the solar system will be used to show the relative distances from the sun of each of the nine planets, along with their locations.

Background

The solar system extends out from the sun to the most distant point on Pluto's orbit, 3,688 million miles away (5,900 million kilometers). The information on the chart below can be used to construct a scale model of the solar system.

Planets' Distance from the Sun									
Categories	Mercury	Venus	Earth	Mars	Jupiter	Saturn	Uranus	Neptune	Pluto
Average Distance from Sun in Millions of Miles (Kilometers)	36 (57.9)	68 (108.2)	93 (149.6)	142 (227.9)	486 (778.3)	893 (1,429)	1,797 (2,875)	2,815 (4,504)	3,688 (5,900)
Relative to Earth's	0.4 AU*	0.7 AU	1.0 AU	1.5 AU	5.2 AU	9.6 AU	19.3 AU	30.3 AU	39.7 AU

*AU = Astronomical Unit, average distance between Earth and sun which is 93 million miles (149.6 million kilometers). The data below each planet shows its distance in astronomical units.

Materials

- at least 300 feet (100 m) of heavy string
- six pieces of heavy cardboard, approximately 5 x 8 inches (12.5 x 20 cm)
- three pieces of heavy cardboard, approximately 8 x 10 inches (20 x 25 cm)
- nine metal washers
- meter stick

Preparation

The scale model of the solar system should be prepared by the teacher for the students to use in this activity. Use the information for the astronomical units in the chart above to create the model.

- Write the names of the planets on the cardboard, using the larger pieces for the three most distant planets (*Uranus*, *Neptune*, and *Pluto*).

- Label each planet's card with its average distance from the sun in miles or kilometers.

- Cut the string for each planet, using a scale based on one astronomical unit equal to 1 meter. Examples: Earth's string would be one meter, Mercury's .4 of a meter, and Pluto's 39.7 meters. Using metric measurements will make it easier to construct the scale.

- Attach the strings, as they are cut, to the planet card. Tie a metal washer on the end of each string to avoid its fraying. Wind the string around the card.

#2381 Exploring Mars   6   © *Teacher Created Materials, Inc.*

Comparing Earth and Mars

Where Is Mars? *(cont.)*

Procedure

1. Review the scale model of the solar system created in the activity How Big Is Mars?

2. Explain that today's activity will show the students where Mars is located in relation to all the other eight planets in the solar system.

3. Show the students the planet cards and explain that the length of string represents the distance of each planet from the sun, cut down to a scale.

4. Stretch out the string for Earth and tell the students that the string is only one meter long, but the actual distance from the sun to the Earth is 93 million miles (149.6 million kilometers).

5. Select one student to represent the sun and hold the washer on the Earth string while another student holds the card. Select four more students to stretch out the strings for Mercury, Venus, and Mars, having the "sun" hold the end of the strings of these three planets as well. Let the students form a straight line to compare the distances of these planets from the sun. Explain that the planets do not travel around the sun in a straight line like this but you have lined them up so their distances can be compared.

6. Point out where Mars is in this model. Tell the students that these four planets are called the inner planets.

7. Select another student to stretch out the string for Jupiter. Students will notice that it is much further from the sun than the inner planets and now will realize why they got that name.

8. Tell them that between Mars and Jupiter is the asteroid belt. Scientists think this is leftover material from the beginning of our solar system that never formed into planets. Many think Deimos and Phobos, the tiny moons of Mars were asteroids which came too close to the planet and were captured by its gravity.

9. Take the students to an area outside that is at least 40 meters in length. Stretch out the strings for all the planets, one at a time so students can see each of these distances. Have three students become the sun so each will hold the ends of the strings for three planets.

For Discussion

• Discuss the great distances of the solar system shown in this model and note how much closer Mars and Earth are to the sun than Jupiter and the other planets beyond it. Ask students what they think the sun must look like as one travels farther into the solar system. (*It would become smaller and less bright. From Mars it appears ⅔ the size of the sun we see. By the time one reaches Pluto, it would be only a small bright star.*)

• Tell the students that Pluto's orbit is more elliptical than the other planets and that it actually passes inside the orbit of Neptune. This happened on January 23, 1979, making Neptune the most distant planet until March 15, 1999, when Pluto is outside Neptune's orbit again. The two planets will never collide, however, since they are so far apart.

• Explain that although our solar system seems huge, it is really like a grain of sand on the beach compared to the size of the Milky Way Galaxy, which includes our solar system. On the same scale used in this model, Alpha Centauri, the nearest star to our solar system, would be nearly 200 miles (320 kilometers) away. This is not even close to the outer edge of the Milky Way Galaxy, and there are billions and billions of galaxies in the Universe.

© Teacher Created Materials, Inc.   *#2381 Exploring Mars*

Comparing Earth and Mars

Martian Motion

Overview
Students will conduct a simulation to illustrate why Mars orbits the sun more slowly than Earth does.

Background
The speed of an orbiting body such as a planet, moon, or the Space Shuttle, is governed by its distance from the mass it orbits. The closer it is to the mass, the faster it must orbit or it will be pulled in by the gravity of the mass. This is true for Mars and Earth as they orbit the sun, with Earth moving faster than Mars since it is closer to the sun.

Materials
- half a drinking straw
- two feet (60 cm) of string
- two large rubber washers

Procedure
1. Distribute a straw, string, and two washers to each student. Have them put the string through the straw and tie a washer on each end.
2. They should hold the straw high above their heads and begin spinning the string so the washer spins out as far as possible.
3. They stop spinning, holding the hand with the straw in the same position and slowly pulling down on the washer at the bottom of the straw.
4. Have them observe what happens as the other washer gets closer to the straw.

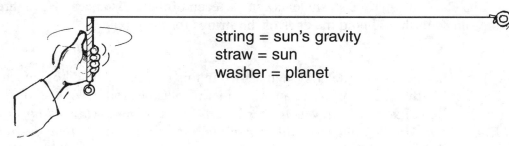

string = sun's gravity
straw = sun
washer = planet

For Discussion
- Discuss what happened as the washer was pulled closer to the straw. (*It began to spin faster around the straw.*)
- Tell the students the information from the background about orbiting bodies.
- Explain that the sun's gravity holds all the planets in their orbits. The straw represents the sun, and the string is the sun's gravity. The washer is a planet in orbit around the sun. As the planet (washer) gets closer to the sun, like the Earth, it must move faster to stay in orbit. If it slows down, it will be pulled into the sun. Mars is farther from the sun than the Earth and thus can travel at a slower speed in its orbit around the sun.

Comparing Earth and Mars

Race of the Planets

Overview

Students will make a flipbook to illustrate the motion of Earth and Mars around the sun.

Background

Earth and Mars orbit the sun at different distances. Since Mars is about $1^1/_2$ times farther from the sun than the Earth, it travels slower in its orbit. Thus, a year on Mars is 687 days, compared to 365 days on Earth. If seen in a time-lapse photograph from beyond the orbits of these planets, they would appear to be in a race with Earth always winning. Mars and Earth would continuously change their distance from each other as they orbit the sun.

Materials

- flipbook pictures (page 12)
- 3" x 5" (7.5 cm x 10 cm) file cards (one for each picture)
- clear packing tape
- transparency of Orbits of the Inner Planets (page 11)
- copy of the Orbits of the Inner Planets for each student
- copy of the data sheet Planet Patterns for each student (page 13)

Preparation

For each student, make sets of the pictures to be used for the flipbook. Depending upon the ability of your students, these may need to be cut in advance.

Procedure (direct instruction by teacher)

1. Show the transparency of the Orbits of the Inner Planets and point out the positions of the orbits of Earth and Mars. Show that Earth is closer to the sun than Mars. Also point out that Mars' orbit is slightly off center from those of the other inner planets.

2. Explain that since Earth is closer, it moves faster around the sun than Mars, so its year is only 365 days, while a year on Mars is 687 days.

3. Show them the 12 positions marked on Earth's orbit and explain that they represent where the Earth will be at the beginning of each of the 12 months. Have the students notice the distance between Earth and Mars in the #1–A position.

4. Explain that when the Earth moves to position #2 in a month, Mars is moving slower so the Earth begins to overtake it. Draw the lines between #2 and B.

5. Connect #3 and C and then #4 and D. Point out that the planets are now very close together. Show that at position 4–D, Mars is on one side of the Earth and the sun is on the other side.

6. Have students predict what will happen when Earth moves to the fifth month. (*It will be farther from Mars and will be pulling ahead of Mars. Mars will therefore seem to fall behind Earth in this race around the sun.*)

7. Continue connecting the numbers and their related letters, discussing what happens. (*Earth continues to get farther from Mars, being most distant at #12 and L.*)

8. Show that Mars has not gone around the sun yet when Earth reaches its starting point #1. Connect the #1 and M positions to show where Earth would be one Earth year later.

© *Teacher Created Materials, Inc.*   9   *#2381 Exploring Mars*

Comparing Earth and Mars

Race of the Planets *(cont.)*

Procedure (student activity)

9. Distribute a set of flipbook pictures to each student. Have them lay the pictures out in order. Let the students compare the drawings with the transparency. Point out that the center circle is the sun, and the two circles around the sun are Mercury and Venus, in that order.

10. Be sure they know the dots represent the planets Mars and Earth. Ask them which dot is Earth (*the one closer to the sun*). Show that the #1 flip picture shows position 1–A on the Orbit of the Planets transparency.

11. Demonstrate how to glue the pictures to the lower left corner of a file card. Help students place the cards in order, with #1 on the top. The cards should now be stacked so their edges are offset about $1/4$ inch (4 mm). Use clear packing tape across the top edge both vertically and horizontally to hold the cards in place.

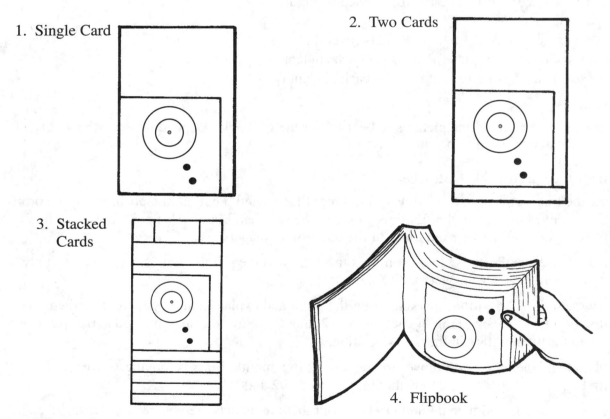

1. Single Card
2. Two Cards
3. Stacked Cards
4. Flipbook

For Discussion

- Have students flip through their books to see Mars and Earth moving around the sun at different speeds.
- Review the transparency with the students so they see the relationship.

Follow Up

Do the Planet Patterns activity to show how the connections between Mars' and Earth's positions in their orbits create an interesting pattern.

#2381 Exploring Mars © Teacher Created Materials, Inc.

Race of the Planets (cont.)

Orbits of the Inner Planets

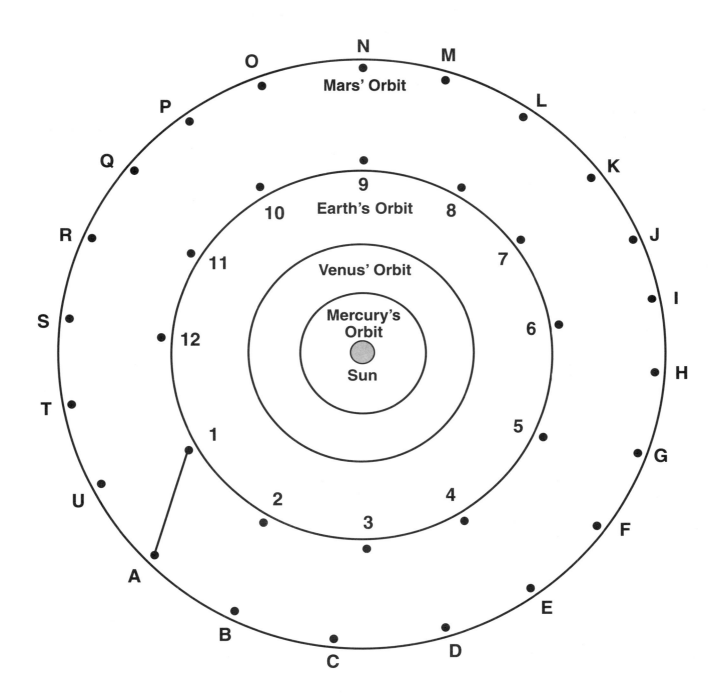

Comparing Earth and Mars

Race of the Planets *(cont.)*

Flipbook Pages

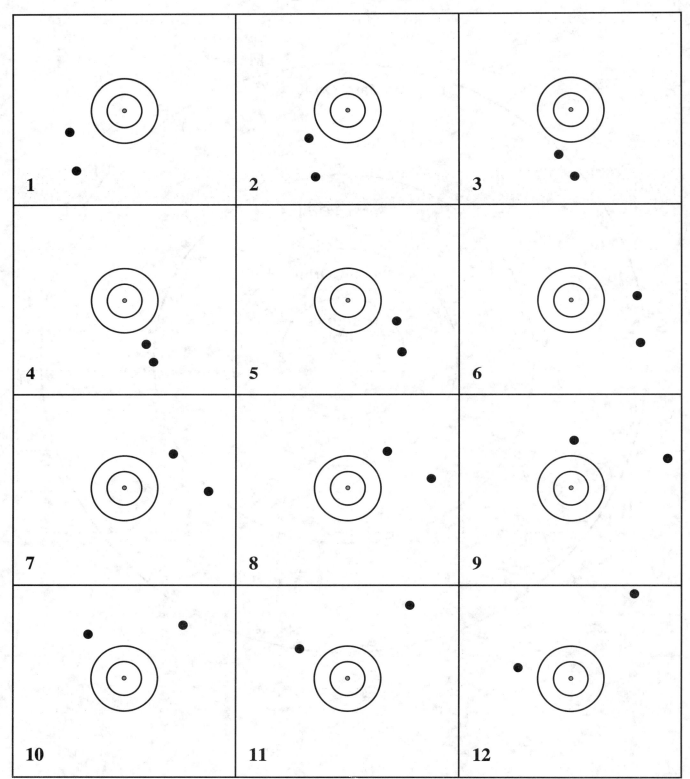

#2381 Exploring Mars 12 © Teacher Created Materials, Inc.

Comparing Earth and Mars

Race of the Planets *(cont.)*

Planet Patterns

To the Students: Use a copy of the Orbits of the Inner Planets to discover the interesting patterns you can make by connecting the positions of Mars and Earth. The first position has been done for you. Continue connecting the dots between Earth and Mars by following the chart below.

Connect the Dots on the Orbits

Cross off each number/letter set when you have drawn the line.

Number to Letter		Number to Letter		Number to Letter	
2	B	1	M	Now it is your turn to complete the pattern.	
3	C	2	N	12	
4	D	3	O		D
5	E	4	P	2	
6	F	5	Q		
7	G	6	R		
8	H	7	S		
9	I	8	T		
10	J	9	U		
11	K	10	A		
12	L	11	B		

Now that you have discovered the pattern of the letters and numbers, you can make your own chart and continue to connect the dots to create a really interesting pattern. Notice how Mars and Earth appear to be dancing back and forth, coming closer and then moving farther apart. This is also shown in the flipbook you made.

© *Teacher Created Materials, Inc.* *#2381 Exploring Mars*

Comparing Earth and Mars

Phases of Earth's Moon

Overview
The students will learn what causes Earth's moon to go through phases.

Background
It takes $27\frac{1}{3}$ days for Earth's moon to make one trip around the planet. We see the moon by reflected sunlight; thus, as it changes position relative to the sun and Earth, it appears to change shape. The changing shapes are called *phases*. Since the Earth is also moving around the sun, it takes $29\frac{1}{2}$ days for the moon to go through all its phases. These phases change continuously throughout the cycle, from no moon visible (new moon) to seeing more of the moon until it becomes fully visible. Gradually, it darkens back to the new phase. This is due to the angle between the observer on Earth and the sunlight striking the moon.

Materials
- sets of Moon Phase Cutouts (page 16)
- envelopes for moon phase sets
- clamp-on light fixture with 150 watt bulb (**Optional:** overhead projector light)
- three-inch (7.5 cm) Styrofoam ball glued to a stick (one for each student)
- transparency of The Phases of the Moon (page 17)

Preparation
- Make enough sets of the Moon Phase Cutouts so students can work in groups of three or four.
- Cut out each set, give each set a number which is written on the back of the phases, and then enclose them in an envelope with the same number as the set.
- Push a stick into the ball about half way and glue around the stick to hold it in place. Clamp the light fixture high up on a wall.

Procedure
1. Ask if students have noticed how the moon appears to change shape. Have them draw the shapes on the board. Explain that this activity will help them understand how the moon changes its shape.

2. Distribute Moon Phase sets to students in small groups. Providing no information, ask them to lay out the phases in proper order to show the full cycle of the moon. Suggest they begin with the black moon and lay the others in a straight line from it.

3. Issue a ball to each student and have them stand around the room, facing the light. Darken the room and turn on the bright light. The ball is the moon and the light is the sun.

5. Demonstrate how to hold the ball in front of their faces as they face the light (blotting out the sun). Have them do this and ask them if they can see the sunlight on the ball. (*No.*) Tell them this phase is called the *new phase*.

6. Ask them to turn counterclockwise slightly. Explain that this is how the moon moves around the Earth—west to east, day after day. Ask if they can see any light on the moon and what shape it reveals. They will see a thin *crescent* moon, illuminated on the right side.

New Moon

Crescent Moon

#2381 Exploring Mars   14   © Teacher Created Materials, Inc.

Comparing Earth and Mars

Phases of Earth's Moon *(cont.)*

7. Have the students turn counterclockwise so they are facing 90 degrees from the sun. Have them again look for the light on the moon. This time they will see the first quarter moon, with only the right side of the moon flooded with light.

First Quarter Moon

8. They rotate slightly further and find that more of the moon is visible now, but not quite all of it. This is the gibbous phase.

Gibbous Moon

9. They continue to move so their backs are to the sun. They must hold the moon above their heads so the shadow does not cut off the sunlight. The view is now of the full moon, for sunlight is shining fully on the side facing the Earth.

Full Moon

10. As the students rotate further, they will find less and less sunlight appearing on the moon. The phases will appear to go in reverse now, with the light on the left side of the moon. These phases are as follows:

Gibbous   **Last Quarter**   **Last Crescent**   **New**

11. Let the students repeat this activity several times as you have them stop and look for the changes of the phases.

For Discussion
- Have the students return to their tables and look at the arrangements of their moon phases. Let them make any changes necessary to put them in the right order.
- Show the students the transparency of the moon's phases and compare that to what they have just seen.

Follow-Up
- Have students begin to look for the moon and make drawings of the shapes they see at the same time each night. A good time to begin this activity is two days after the new moon when the phase is a thin crescent. Be sure students observe about half an hour after sunset so they can see the moon is not only changing shape but also moving eastward each night.
- Do the next activity simulating the phases of Deimos, one of the two moons of Mars.

Comparing Earth and Mars

Phases of Earth's Moon *(cont.)*

Moon Phase Cutouts

To the Teacher: The moon phases shown below are to be copied to make sets for each group of students. Cut out each set of phases and number them as separate sets to avoid mixing them. Enclose them in envelopes with the same number on them as the set inside.

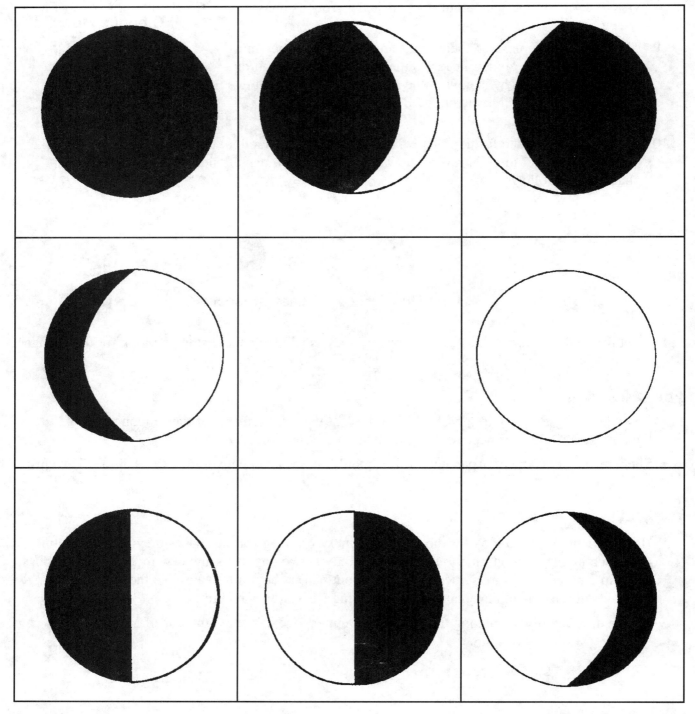

#2381 Exploring Mars © Teacher Created Materials, Inc.

Phases of Earth's Moon *(cont.)*

The Phases of the Moon

The outer circle of positions shows how the moon appears from space. The inner circle of positions shows the different phases of the moon as it appears from Earth.

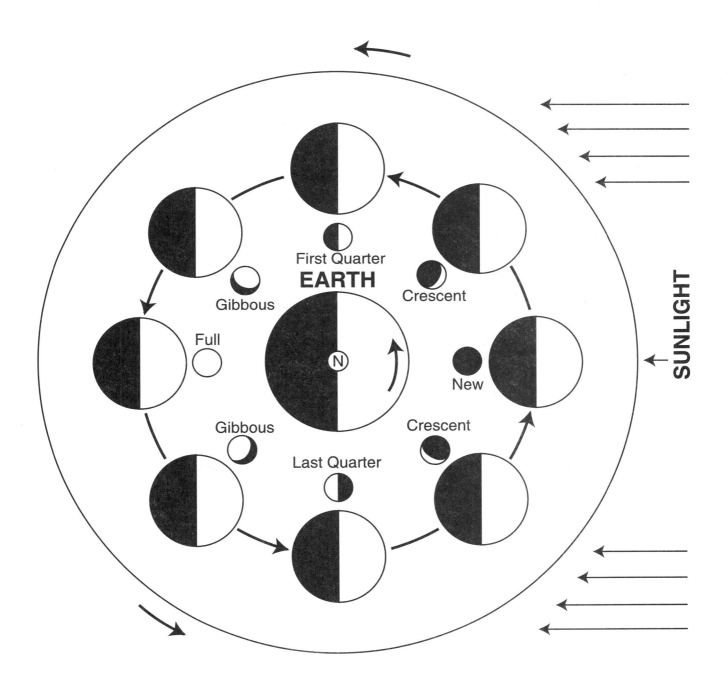

Comparing Earth and Mars

Martian Moons

Overview

Students will simulate the phases of Deimos, one of the moons of Mars.

Background

In 1610 Johannes Kepler predicted that Mars might have two satellites, based on the fact that Earth has one and Galileo had seen four moons around Jupiter. It was just a wild guess, but it probably influenced Jonathan Swift in his 1726 book *Gulliver's Travels* when he wrote of two lesser stars or satellites revolving around Mars. But these two satellites were not actually seen until 1877. Asaph Hall, their discoverer, named the two tiny worlds Deimos (terror) and Phobos (fear) after the guard dogs of Mars, the Roman god of war.

These Martian moons orbit very close to their planet. Phobos, the closer moon, takes only 7 hours and 39 minutes to circle Mars once. This tiny, odd-shaped satellite is about 17 x 14 x 12 miles (27 x 22 x 19 km). Deimos, farther from Mars, orbits the planet in 30 hours 18 minutes. It is even smaller than Phobos, being 9 x 7.5 x 7 miles (15 x 12 x 11 km). Both moons are shaped somewhat like a Russet potato, even having craters like the potato's depressions.

Because Phobos orbits the planet in less time than one Martian day (24.5 hours), it crosses the sky twice daily, moving west to east, the same direction as Earth's moon. Deimos takes a little longer than the Martian day to orbit the planet in the same direction. The speed with which these two moons move around Mars would create a unique view for the Martian observer. Phobos would look somewhat like a race horse when both moons are in the sky, as it would catch up to Deimos and pass it. The same face of the Martian moons always faces the planet. This means the moons rotate around their axes at the same speed they revolve around Mars, just as Earth's moon does.

Deimos is too small and too far away from Mars to cause a solar eclipse. When it does pass between Mars and the sun, anyone standing on Mars would see Deimos as an irregularly-shaped black object silhouetted against the bright solar disc. Phobos, however, can cast a shadow on Mars. If an observer were standing on the Martian surface within the path of the shadow, he would see the sun eclipsed, just as the Moon eclipses the sun on Earth. But because of the rapid motion of Phobos, the eclipse would last for about one second only. The longest a solar eclipse can last on Earth is a little over seven minutes.

Materials

- Russet potato for each student
- sharpened pencil for each potato
- clamp-on light fixture with 150-watt bulb (**Optional:** overhead projector light)
- copy of Observing the Martian Moons (page 20) for each student

Preparation

- Push a sharpened pencil into the center of each potato.
- Clamp the light high up on the wall.

#2381 Exploring Mars   18   © *Teacher Created Materials, Inc.*

Comparing Earth and Mars

Martian Moons *(cont.)*

Procedure

1. Review the phases-of-the-moon activity to remind students of the way the light caused the phases to occur.

2. Explain appropriate background information about the two moons of Mars.

3. Issue each student a potato on a pencil and explain that it will represent Deimos, the smaller and more distant moon of Mars.

4. Turn off all the lights except the 150-watt bulb. Remind the students that this represents the sun, which would actually appear $2/3$ smaller from Mars than it does from Earth.

5. Have them face the sun and hold one of the pointed ends of the potato between their faces and the sun.

6. Tell them to slowly rotate counterclockwise (west-to-east) and watch to see how the light changes on Deimos, always keeping the same end of the moon facing them.

7. Have students describe what they see as they look at Deimos throughout the rotation. (*It will appear to go through phases like Earth's moon but will not be as clear to see due to the irregularly shaped surface.*)

8. Have the students form groups of three, with one student representing Mars and the other two representing Deimos and Phobos.

9. Mars should rotate slowly, while Phobos orbits twice for each rotation and Deimos about once for each rotation.

Follow-Up

• Review the activity Martian Motion they did earlier to simulate the motions of Earth and Mars around the sun. Help them see that the same concept applies to the speed of Deimos and Phobos as they orbit Mars.

• Have students complete the worksheet Observing the Martian Moons (page 20).

Answers to Observing the Martian Moons:

Students should be able to describe Deimos and Phobos as potato-shaped moons, with Deimos being the smaller and more distant moon. The picture should show Phobos larger than Deimos. They should appear as irregularly shaped circles. Some students may also show the phases. With the sun just setting in the west, the phase will depend upon the position of the moon relative to the sun, just as it did when doing the simulation.

Comparing Earth and Mars

Martian Moons *(cont.)*

Observing the Martian Moons

To the Student: You are an astronomer who has just arrived on Mars. The first thing you want to do is to observe the night sky from Mars. Like all scientists, you make an observation log which records information such as what time you observed. You also make a detailed drawing of what you saw in the sky.

Your picture and notes are not finished yet. Add information about the moons Deimos and Phobos and then draw them in the sky.

Observing Log

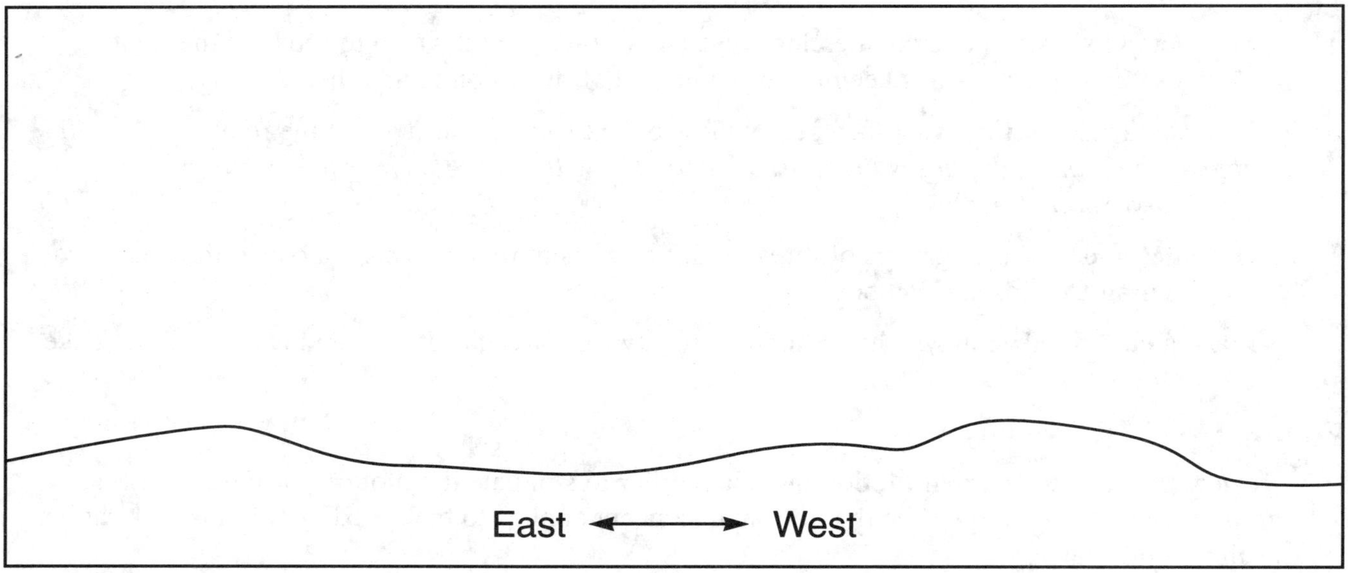

East ←——→ West

Time: 7:00 p.m.

Direction: Facing South

Sky Conditions: Clear skies, sun has just set in the west, Deimos and Phobos visible.

Description of Moons: _____

_____

_____

_____

_____

_____

#2381 Exploring Mars   20   © *Teacher Created Materials, Inc.*

Comparing Earth and Mars

How's the Weather Up There?

Overview

Students will do a variety of activities designed to help them compare seasons, temperatures, and air pressure on Earth and Mars.

Reasons for the Seasons

Background

The concept of seasonal changes is very abstract. Most students (and many adults) believe that seasons are due to the changes in distance between Earth and the sun at different times of the year. Although this distance does vary, it is not the cause of the seasons. These are caused by unequal amounts of sunlight reaching various parts of the Earth due to the tilt of its axis. Earth's axis, an imaginary line running through the center of the planet and connecting the north and south poles, tilts at $23\frac{1}{2}$ degrees to our path around the sun. Four seasons are the result of this tilt—winter, spring, summer, and fall. The tilt also is responsible for the fact that the northern and southern hemispheres experience opposite seasons, due to the changes in the angle of the sunlight hitting the planet during our 365-day journey.

Mars' axis tilts 25 degrees; thus it also experiences four seasons, with opposite seasons in the hemispheres—just like Earth. Since a year on Mars is 687 days, its seasons last about 81 days longer than Earth's. Scientists have discovered that during summer in the northern hemisphere of Mars, weather is fairly quiet, but dust storms are common during the southern summers. Mars' elliptical orbit brings it closer to the sun during summer in the southern hemisphere, so it is hotter than summer in the northern hemisphere, a time when the planet is farther from the sun.

When the Mars *Pathfinder* landed on Mars on July 4, 1997, in the northern hemisphere, it was summer just as it was on Earth. Fall was approaching, just as on Earth, and the Martian weather system with winds from the west would be bringing dust storms.

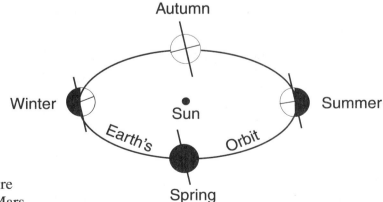

Seasons Seen from Outer Space

Materials

- large globe
- 10 large toothpicks
- clamp-on 150-watt light fixture
- location flags for Earth and Mars
- Signs for the Seasons Activity (page 24)
- removable adhesive putty used to hang pictures
- ball which is about $\frac{1}{2}$ the size of the globe to represent Mars
- star cut from 3 x 5 inch (7.5 cm x 10 cm) file card

© Teacher Created Materials, Inc.   21   #2381 Exploring Mars

Comparing Earth and Mars

How's the Weather Up There? *(cont.)*

Reasons for the Seasons *(cont.)*

Preparation

- Copy the Signs for the Seasons Activity on heavy paper. Cut these pieces out.
- Find a room such as the cafeteria, which can be darkened and will provide a large empty space for this activity.
- Draw Earth's orbit using a string two feet (60 cm) long for the radius. Mark the circle with chalk or washable pen. Place the season signs at 90 degree angle points inside this circle.
- Draw another circle with a radius of three feet (120 cm) to represent Mars' orbit around the sun. Have the center of this circle be about two inches off that of Earth's. Make a collar from a strip of cardboard to support the ball on the floor.
- Clamp the light to a low chair in the center of Earth's orbit so it is the same level as the equator on the globe.
- Tape the location flags to ends of the toothpicks. Use the adhesive putty to fix them to the globe and Mars ball in correct locations. These need to be in a straight line from pole to pole. The toothpicks should point toward the centers of the planets.
- Hang the paper star from the ceiling just beyond the winter spot on Earth's orbit. This serves as a target for the North Pole end of the axis for both planets.
- Put the globe in the winter position, pointing the North Pole towards the North Star hanging from the ceiling.

Procedure

1. Ask the students to draw an explanation for the seasons. Have them share their ideas in small groups and then save these ideas to reevaluate after they do the activity.

2. Take the students to the room where the activity will be conducted. Position them on the summer side of the orbit so they can clearly see the Earth at winter.

3. Explain that the light will represent the sun and the globe is the Earth. Show the location of the six flags on the globe and tell them these will help them see the angle of the sun at different locations on the Earth during the various seasons.

4. Point out the circle which is the path the Earth follows around the sun, in a counterclockwise motion. Show them the seasonal positions and explain that the dates show when these seasons begin, but they gradually change from one to the other.

5. Turn on the bright light and turn off the room lights. Spin the Earth to first demonstrate day and night. This will help students see the difference between the daily and annual motions that Earth experiences.

6. Set the globes with the flags in the light. Show that the sun's light is not shining directly on the northern hemisphere and that the flags north of the equator show longer shadows closer to the North Pole. Point out that everything north of the Arctic Circle is in shadow, and thus the sun would not be above the horizon any part of the day. It is winter here.

7. Have them compare this to the southern hemisphere. Light is shining more directly, and the toothpick shadows are shorter. The South Pole is receiving light all day. It is summer here.

#2381 Exploring Mars   22   © *Teacher Created Materials, Inc.*

Comparing Earth and Mars

How's the Weather Up There? *(cont.)*

Reasons for the Seasons *(cont.)*

Procedure *(cont.)*

8. Move the globe to the spring position, carrying it so the North Pole always points toward the North Star. Move the students to the fall position. Show them that sunlight is shining directly on the equator and that both northern and southern hemispheres are receiving equal amounts of sunlight. The shadows of the toothpicks should be about equal length for the same latitudes in north and south. It is spring north of the equator and fall south of it.

9. Move the globe to the summer position and students to the winter location. The northern hemisphere is receiving direct light; it is summer here. The southern hemisphere's light is indirect; it is winter here.

10. Move the globe to the fall position and students to spring, and compare how this is different from the spring location. The sun is again directly over the equator, with equal amounts of light reaching both hemispheres. It is fall north of the equator and spring south of it.

For Discussion

- Repeat the demonstration, asking the students questions to help them make closer observations. Examples are given below.

  Winter: Where are toothpick shadows longest? (*northern hemisphere*)

  Summer: What season is the northern hemisphere having? How do you know? (*Sunlight is shining directly on this area.*) What season is it south of the equator? (*winter*)

  Spring and Fall: Where is the direct sunlight on Earth? (*equator*)

- Ask students if they see why the angle of sunlight changes as the Earth rotates. (*The Earth is tilted so different areas are turned to the light as it orbits the sun.*) Be sure students see the North Pole always points the same direction as it orbits the sun.

- Place the ball representing Mars on its orbit opposite the summer position. Place Earth in this same location on its orbit. Point out that Mars tilts about the same angle as Earth and thus also has seasons. The North Pole of Mars points in the general direction of the North Star. Show the shadows of the toothpicks on the surface of Mars and compare them to Earth, also in the summer position. They should see that on both planets the northern hemisphere is receiving more direct sunlight (*shadows get shorter moving north from the equator*). The southern hemispheres are receiving indirect light and thus are colder; these areas are having winter.

- Move Mars to the other seasonal positions, traveling counterclockwise, just as Earth does. Stop to compare the sun's location and shadows at each position for Earth and Mars. Explain that since Mars travels slower than Earth, each of its seasons are about 81 days longer than Earth's.

Follow-Up

- Have students draw another picture to explain the seasons. Have them compare it with the one they did before doing this activity.

© *Teacher Created Materials, Inc.*   23   *#2381 Exploring Mars*

Comparing Earth and Mars

How's the Weather Up There? *(cont.)*

Signs for the Seasons Activity

Los Angeles 34°N	Tropic of Cancer 23½°N	South Pacific 34°S	South Pole 90°S

Tropic of Capricorn 23½°S	Equator 0°	North Pole 90°N

Winter
Northern Hemisphere
December 21

Spring
Northern Hemisphere
March 20

Summer
Northern Hemisphere
June 21

Fall
Northern Hemisphere
September 23

Mars Equator 0°	Mars North Pole 90°N	Mars South Pole 90°S

Pathfinder Landing Site 19°N 3°W

#2381 Exploring Mars — 24 — © Teacher Created Materials, Inc.

Comparing Earth and Mars

How's the Weather Up There? *(cont.)*

Temperatures

Background

A variety of conditions control temperatures on Earth and Mars. The average distance of Earth from the sun is 93 million miles (150 million km), but Mars' average is 142 million miles (228 million km). This greater distance means less sunlight is reaching Mars, creating colder extremes in temperatures than those on Earth. Temperatures on both planets get colder as one moves from the equator to the poles. On Mars, extremes in temperatures can be -199 degrees F (-128 degrees C) during polar nights to 80 degrees F (27 degrees C) at the equator, at noon, when the planet is closest to the sun. Temperature extremes on Earth have been recorded from -129 degrees F (-90 degrees C) in Antarctica to 136 degrees F (58 degrees C) in North Africa. The atmosphere on Mars is also much thinner than on Earth. Mars has less mass and thus less gravity to hold as much atmosphere as Earth can. This permits heat to leave Mars' surface faster at night than it does on Earth.

Materials

- eight outdoor thermometers (all the same type)
- three cardboard tubes (from toilet tissue rolls)
- 24 6-oz. cups (30 mL)
- ice
- hot water
- masking tape
- transparency and seven copies of Temperature Records data sheet (page 27)
- transparency and seven copies of Temperature Graph (page 28)

Preparation

- After teaching students how to read the thermometers, tape one thermometer to each of the north, east, west, and south sides of the school building.
- Make a transparency of the thermometer. This can be done by placing it on a copier and following the normal procedure to make a transparency.
- Plan on dividing students into eight groups for this activity. Each group will need a set of cups half-full of hot, cold, and room temperature water. The cups should be labeled according to the type of water in each (i.e., hot, cold, etc.).

Procedure

1. Divide students into eight groups. Distribute a thermometer to each group.
2. Use the thermometers and transparency to help students learn how to read them.
3. Distribute the set of three different temperatures of water to each group.
4. Let them place their thermometers in the room-temperature water and record the temperatures on a piece of paper. Monitor their progress to be sure they are correct.
5. Have them find the temperatures of the cold and hot water and record them on paper. Check for accuracy. Discuss what they saw happen to the liquid in the thermometers as they placed them in different temperatures. (*The liquid drops in cold, climbs in hot, and is somewhere in between for room temperature water.*)

© *Teacher Created Materials, Inc.*   25   *#2381 Exploring Mars*

Comparing Earth and Mars

How's the Weather Up There? *(cont.)*

Temperatures *(cont.)*

Procedure *(cont.)*

6. Early the next morning after introducing the temperatures, divide the students into eight groups. Introduce the temperature record to each group. Assign two groups to each of the four areas to read the thermometers, providing double readings for each location as a check.

7. Take the students outside to find the locations of the thermometers you have placed around the building and near the door. Let each group record their data and then return to the classroom.

8. Write the students' data for all four locations on a transparency of the record sheet.

For Discussion

• Discuss the differences students found in the north, south, east, and west locations and why they occur. (*position of the sun*)

• Assign members of the groups to various times throughout the day when they are to report to their respective weather stations and read the thermometers. The two students assigned to the same thermometers should agree on their readings.

Follow-Up

• Collect the data from each group at the end of the day. Write the data on the transparency of the record sheet.

• Make a graph of the data on the transparency of the graph. Use a different color for each of the four different directions.

• On the next day, show the transparency of the temperature readings compiled from the previous day's data gathered by the eight groups. Explain that each group will graph its own temperature data which was collected the day before.

• Distribute the Temperature Record data sheets to each group. Demonstrate how to plot the first two data on their graphs. Monitor their progress as they complete their line graphs.

• Show the graph you have made of the four locations. Discuss the differences and have students offer explanations of why they are not the same throughout the day. (*Position of sunlight changes during the day as it moves across the sky and changes height in the sky.*)

• Share the background comparing the temperatures of Earth and Mars, as is appropriate for your students. Be sure to explain why there are such differences between the temperatures on these two planets.

#2381 Exploring Mars 26 *© Teacher Created Materials, Inc.*

How's the Weather Up There? *(cont.)*

Temperatures *(cont.)*

Temperature Records

Direction	8 A.M.	9 A.M.	10 A.M.	11 A.M.	12 P.M.	1 P.M.	2 P.M.	3 P.M.
North	°	°	°	°	°	°	°	°
South	°	°	°	°	°	°	°	°
East	°	°	°	°	°	°	°	°
West	°	°	°	°	°	°	°	°

Comparing Earth and Mars

How's the Weather Up There? *(cont.)*

Temperature Graph

To the Students: Plot the data from your group's Temperature Record on the graph below and then connect the dots to make a line graph.

Direction:_____

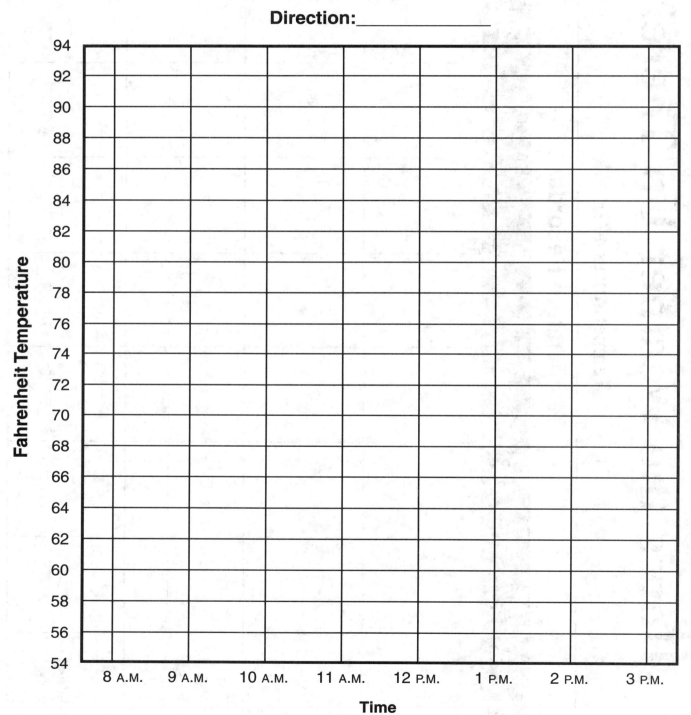

#2381 Exploring Mars 28 © Teacher Created Materials, Inc.

Comparing Earth and Mars

How's the Weather Up There? *(cont.)*

Air Pressure

Overview

Students will do an experiment to simulate the difference in air pressure on Mars from that on Earth.

Background

The atmosphere on Earth creates air pressure of 14.7 pounds per square inch (1.03 kg per square centimeter) at sea level. The atmosphere is much thinner on Mars, and thus the air pressure is lower. At ground level on Mars, the air pressure is only .1 pounds per square inch (.007 kg per square centimeter).

Materials (for each student)

- 8 1/2 x 11 inch (21 x 27.5 cm) graph paper (Use 1" or 1 cm.)
- 2-inch (5 x 5 cm) square of 1" or 1 cm graph paper
- two small rubber bands
- two pieces of clear tape

Procedure

1. Distribute the materials to each student. Have them tape a rubber band in the centers of the large and small papers.
2. Tell the students that although they do not feel the weight of the atmosphere against them, it is really pressing at 14.7 pounds for every square inch (2.5 cm) on their body.
3. Point out that the graph paper shows square inches (centimeters) and will be used to show them just how much pressure this is.
4. Have them flatten the larger paper on their table so no air bubbles are under it.
5. Tell them that when you give a signal, they should pull the paper up as fast as they can, using the rubber band.
6. Tell them to place a finger through the rubber band and wait for your signal.
7. Give the signal and have the students pull up on the paper. Let them discuss what happened. (*The paper was pushed down so hard by the air that it makes a sucking noise as it is pulled up.*)
8. Repeat this with the smaller paper.

For Discussion

- Tell the students that the smaller paper gave them some idea of how much less air pressure there is from Mars' atmosphere. If the paper were the same size as the larger one and were placed on a table on Mars, it would be as easy to pull as the small one was here on Earth.
- Explain that animals that live on the land have evolved so that their bodies push out with a pressure equal to that of the air pressing against them. Give the example of what happens if you were to go diving into the deepest areas of the ocean. We would be crushed because of the tremendous pressure of the water pushing on our bodies.
- Tell them that animals do live in these depths on the ocean floor. They have evolved to adjust to the pressure and would explode if brought to the surface where the pressure is much lower.
- Ask students what would happen to our bodies if we were to step out on the surface of Mars where the air pressure is much less than on Earth. (*Our bodies would explode since the air pressure inside them is pushing out at Earth's pressure.*)

© Teacher Created Materials, Inc. 29 *#2381 Exploring Mars*

Comparing Earth and Mars

How's the Weather Up There? *(cont.)*

Weather Report

Overview
Students compare weather reports from Earth with those from Mars.

Background
Following is the weather data gathered at the Carl Sagan Memorial Station, the landing site of Mars *Pathfinder*, on July 31, 1997.

- Pressure 6.71 millibars and falling (*Earth is usually about 1,000 millibars. Falling air pressure often means storms if it is falling rapidly.*)
- Expected cool daytime temperature 10° F (-12° C) and night temperature -105° F (-76° C)
- Winds light from the west, night and morning pink clouds and sky
- No rain expected ever!
- At sunset a white sun was surrounded by pink sky, fading to black.

Materials
- weather pages from daily newspaper
- video clips of weather reports on TV

Preparation
- Videotape excerpts of weather reports from various TV channels.
- Assign students to bring in the weather page from their newspapers.

Procedure
1. Have students share the information gathered about the weather.
2. Show transparencies of weather maps from a series of three consecutive days. Have students observe the direction of the frontal movements across the United States (west to east).
3. View the excerpts from the TV reports.
4. Post samples of the weather pages on a bulletin board.

For Discussion
- Give the weather report from Mars for July 31, 1997.
- Give the most recent online weather report from Mars. (See Resources for Web sites, page 79.)
- Have students compare Martian weather with that on Earth.

Follow-Up
Explain that winds are deflected in a clockwise pattern north of the equator and counterclockwise south of the equator. This is due to Earth's rotation west to east. Mars rotates in the same direction, so its wind patterns are like those on Earth. The Mars *Pathfinder*'s landing site is north of Mars' equator, explaining the winds out of the west.

You can demonstrate this by using a globe and washable felt pen. (Test the pen on a small area of the globe first to be sure it will wash off.)

- Set the globe on a table where all students can see it. Begin to rotate it west to east.
- While spinning the globe, place the pen at the north pole and quickly draw at least six straight lines toward the equator. Lift the pen and return to the pole for each new line.
- When the globe stops, the lines will appear to curve in a clockwise direction. Spin the globe again but draw the lines from the south pole. The lines will now appear to curve counterclockwise.

#2381 Exploring Mars
30
© Teacher Created Materials, Inc.

Mars Pathfinder Mission

Build Your Own Microrover

Overview

The teacher will construct a full-sized model of the *Sojourner* microrover which landed on Mars, July 4, 1997.

Background

The Planetary Society and Jet Propulsion Laboratory (JPL) of Pasadena conducted a worldwide contest in 1995 to find a name for the small rover that was being constructed to be sent to Mars. Anyone 18 years or younger could participate. Out of the 3,500 entries, 12-year-old Valerie Ambroise from Bridgeport, Connecticut, submitted the winning name. She suggested the rover be named *Sojourner,* which means "one who stays for a brief time—a visitor." It was also the name of a Civil War era abolitionist and champion for women's rights, Sojourner Truth, who traveled the country advocating the rights of all people to be free.

The *Sojourner* rover is not much larger than a small microwave oven. It is about two feet (60 cm) long and one foot (30 cm) high. It weighs about 38.5 pounds (17.5 kg) on Earth but only about 22 pounds (10 kg) on Mars, due to less gravity on that planet. It has six individually motorized wheels, which are cleated for better traction. Each wheel moves independently of the others.

Solar panels cover the top surface of the rover to supply the energy it needs to move. Since bright sunlight is needed for the solar panels to generate energy, they can only operate during the Martian day (about 10:00 A.M. to 2 P.M. PT). The Mars rover has an x-ray spectrometer, which can be extended to "sniff" the rocks and analyze their chemical make-up. It also has two black and white cameras in front for a stereoscopic view (just like having two eyes) and a color camera in the rear. Five lasers across the front of the vehicle have overlapping beams which act as eyes to detect anything which might be in its path, such as a cliff or large rock. When an obstacle is found, the rover stops until it receives commands from scientists on Earth.

Materials

- drawings for model (page 33)
- foam board at least two feet square (60 cm sq.), blue on one side (or spray paint dark blue)
- serrated knife to cut foam board
- circles of Styrofoam 5–6 inches (12.5–15 cm) in diameter and 2 inches (5 cm) thick. If necessary, two 1-inch (2.5 cm) thick circles can be glued together (available from florists or craft supply stores).
- $^1/_4$ inch (0.5 cm) x 1 foot (30 cm) wooden dowel
- cardboard box or Styrofoam blocks which can be used to form the warm electronic box, approximately 6 inches (15 cm) thick, 20 inches (50 cm) long, 14 inches (35 cm) wide
- gold and silver spray paint
- six wooden sticks (Tongue depressors will work.)
- glue gun or other strong glue
- two nails at least $2^1/_2$ inches (6.5 cm) long
- electric drill
- transparency of Mars Microrover *Sojourner* (page 34)
- Mars Microrover Information (page 35)

© *Teacher Created Materials, Inc.*   31   *#2381 Exploring Mars*

Mars Pathfinder Mission

Build Your Own Microrover *(cont.)*

Materials *(cont.)*

Optional: Scale model of the Mars *Pathfinder* produced by Hot Wheels of Mattel—a $^1/_{64}$th scale model of the Mars *Pathfinder* cruise spacecraft, lander, and rover. Call Mattel at (800)524-TOYS for information about stores carrying this model.

Preparation (Instructions for building model)

- Spray the wooden dowel (antenna), wheels, and sticks silver. Spray the electronic box gold.
- Draw the dimensions of the solar panels shown in the top view of *Sojourner* (page 33) on the foam board. Use a serrated knife to cut it. Glue the solar panel to the top of the gold electronic box.
- Drill a small hole near the front of the solar panel, to one side (see picture).
- Force the wooden dowel into the hole and glue it in place.
- Drill holes in four sticks to attach them with the long nails on both sides of the electronic box as shown in the drawing. Glue them to hold them in place securely. Glue the other sticks to one of these sticks on each side of the box as shown.
- Glue the wheels to the sticks as shown.
- Glue small items to the electronic box to represent the spectrometer and camera in the rear and two cameras and five lasers in the front of the rover. These should be placed under the solar panels as shown in the drawing.

Discussion

- Share the information about how the Mars rover *Sojourner* was named.
- Show the transparency of the rover (page 34) and share the appropriate information.
- Show the model of the *Sojourner* and compare it to this picture.

Follow Up

Sojourner used two cameras to provide a stereoscopic view that is relayed to JPL on Earth via the Mars *Pathfinder* lander. Students can do a simple experiment with their own eyes to see how they work together to provide an in-depth view.

- Tell the students to look at an object on the wall of the classroom (e.g., the clock).
- Have them close one eye and extend their closed fists, thumbs up. Tell them to cover the clock with their thumbs.
- While holding their thumb in the same spot, tell them to slowly blink one eye and then the other. The object will appear to move back and forth.

Explanation: Our eyes are separated from each other, and thus we receive two views from slightly different angles. The brain combines these two images into one. This provides us with a view in which we see objects at different distances. If we had only one eye, we would lose much of our depth perception and the view would appear flattened. The effect of this can be experienced by tossing a ball back and forth with a partner, and then repeating this with a patch over one eye.

#2381 Exploring Mars   *© Teacher Created Materials, Inc.*

Build Your Own Microrover (cont.)

Mars Rover

Top View

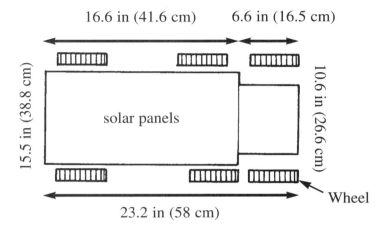

The wheels are each 1.6 inches (4 cm) wide and 5 inches (12.5 cm) in diameter. The microrover is 12.8 inches (32 cm) high.

Side View

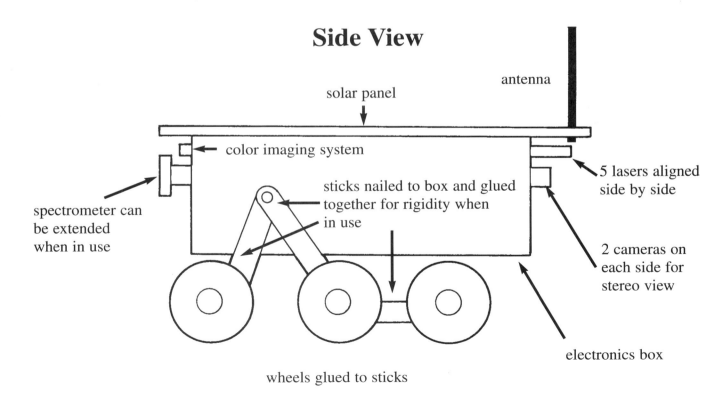

Mars Pathfinder Mission

Build Your Own Microrover *(cont.)*

Mars Microrover *Sojourner*

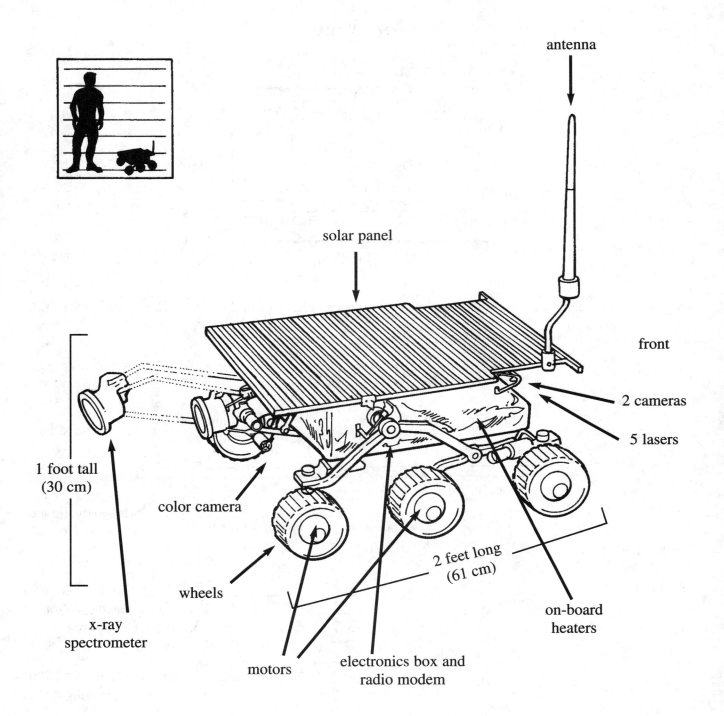

Mars Pathfinder Mission

Build Your Own Microrover *(cont.)*

Mars Microrover Information

To the Teacher: Select information which is appropriate for your students and share it as they view the transparency of the *Sojourner* Rover shown on the previous page.

The *Viking 1* and *2* missions (1975–1982) cost $3 billion (in 1997 dollars) for two launches, two orbiters, and two landers. The *Pathfinder* mission cost $250 million for launcher, lander, and rover. It took eight years to develop the *Vikings* and only four years for the *Pathfinder*.

Mars *Pathfinder* landed 525 miles away from where *Viking I* landed on June 1976, 21 years earlier.

The *Sojourner* has been called the "Bargain-Basement Rover." It was constructed with mostly available parts, rather than spending money to develop new ones specifically for this mission as had been done with *Viking*. It is also much less sophisticated than the *Viking 1* and *2* landers. The rover is designed to last up to a month. *Viking* lasted six years. The rover's only task is to analyze the rocks and soil on Mars; therefore, it is mostly a geology mission.

Cameras—Two front-mounted black-and-white cameras, separated to take two images that provide a stereoscopic view. A single rear-mounted camera takes color pictures.

Electronics—The brain of the rover is a tiny eight-bit Intel 80C85 processor chosen for its ruggedness and its low cost. The processor contains only 6,500 transistors, compared with 5.5 million in a top-of-the-line Pentium chip.

Laser navigation—Five lasers help steer the rover by laying down a path and identifying obstructions. These lasers are mounted on the front and overlap to provide information to guide the rover around obstacles.

Motors—Miniature electric motors mounted in each wheel push the craft forward at top speeds of two feet per minute (120 feet per hour)

On-board heaters—Three heaters inside rover's electronic box keep this area warm. Temperatures on Ares Vallis, the rover's location on Mars, fluctuate between -65 degrees F at night to 10 degrees F by daybreak. Each heater is the size of a flashlight battery and is nuclear powered by an extremely small amount of radioactive material—plutonium 238.

Radio modem—Even when it works right, this bulky radio modem sends signals only at a sluggish 9,600 bits per second.

Solar panel—*Sojourner* is powered during the Martian day by more than 200 razor-thin photovoltaic cells. The rover also carries nine lithium D-cell batteries, but to save money, the batteries are not rechargeable.

Wheels—Six 5-inch (12.5 cm) independently mounted wheels can adapt to the terrain. They can climb over rocks as high as 10 inches (25.4 cm). Six wheels were used rather than four to add stability to the rover.

X-ray spectrometer—This device will stretch out and "sniff" rocks and soil to analyze the chemicals found in them.

© *Teacher Created Materials, Inc.*   35   *#2381 Exploring Mars*

Mars Pathfinder Mission

Slower Than a Speeding Snail

Overview
Students will simulate the motion of the *Sojourner* rover to see how slowly it moves.

Background
The *Sojourner* moves at a top speed of two feet (60 cm) per minute, about 0.4 inches (1 cm) per second. This slow pace gives the five lasers time to see any problems well in advance so *Sojourner* will be shut down and not roll off a cliff or bump into a rock. The lasers can also detect when the rover may tip. It stays near the lander within an area the size of a football field. It can go up a 30-degree slope and scale eight-inch (20 cm) rocks.

On Sol 2 (the scientific term for day two on Mars) the *Sojourner* rolled down the ramp and onto the dusty soil of Mars. It "sniffed" the dust at the end of the ramp with its x-ray spectrometer. The test showed the dust was rich in iron and almost exactly like the soil tested by the *Viking* landers in 1976. This means that Mars' topsoil may be widely spread over the planet due to dust storms. In 1971 images of Mars taken by the unmanned *Mariner 9* spacecraft orbiting the planet showed a dust storm with winds traveling at 315 mph (504 kph) and spreading across the entire planet.

Next, the small rover was sent out to investigate a rock that scientists named Barnacle Bill (BB) since it looked as if it were covered with barnacles. This 10-inch (26 cm) high rock was about an arm's length from the lander. When the spectrometer was used on BB, the rock was found to be loaded with quartz. This was a surprise since quartz found on Earth results from rocks being melted and solidified many times by volcanism or crustal plate movement. Mars seems to have very few volcanoes, however, and shows no signs of crustal plate moving. Scientists now realize that the geology on Mars is more complex than expected. The chemicals *Sojourner* found in BB were nearly identical to those of the 12 meteorites found in 1984 in Antarctica which are believed to have come from Mars.

Materials
- meter sticks or metric tape measures
- small match boxes or model cards to represent the rover
- timer with digital readout of seconds
- two small file cards—one marked START, the other STOP
- model of *Sojourner* (constructed in Build Your Own Microrover)
- 15 feet (5 m) of string marked at one-foot (30 cm) intervals with a black felt pen

Preparation
- Have one of the students demonstrate how far he or she can walk in a minute. Give the person the end of the 15-foot string and have him or her walk in a straight line, unraveling the string along the way. Time the student for one minute and then measure the string to see how far he or she traveled.

- Tell the students about *Sojourner's* speed over the surface of Mars. Explain that they are going to do an experiment to see just how fast it moved.

- Divide the students into groups of three or four and distribute a measuring device, matchbox or car, and a pair of cards to each group.

#2381 Exploring Mars　　　36　　　© *Teacher Created Materials, Inc.*

Mars Pathfinder Mission

Slower Than a Speeding Snail *(cont.)*

Procedure

1. Have the students lay out the meter stick on a bare floor or pavement. If a tape measure is used, hold it in place with tape, being sure the centimeter numbers are visible.
2. Tell students to place the START card at the beginning of the measuring device and tape it to the table. Place the STOP card at the 60-centimeter location and tape it in place.
3. Share the information about the speed with which the *Sojourner* rover can move on Mars.
4. Inform the students that they are about to do an experiment to see just how fast that speed is.
5. Tell them that they will use the box (model car) to represent the rover. They should place it on the START card at the beginning of the measuring device.
6. Explain that as you count off 60 seconds, they are to move the rover forward alongside the measuring device, one centimeter for each count. They should have their rover on the same number centimeter as the second you call out so they can keep up with the speed.
7. State, "Ready, begin." Then start counting off the seconds from the digital readout. Say "Stop" when you reach 60 seconds.
8. If time permits, repeat this activity with other members of the group moving the rover.

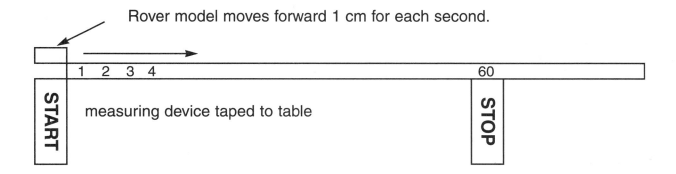

For Discussion

Discuss what the students thought about the speed of the *Sojourner*. Be sure they know why it had to move so slowly. *(to provide time for its lasers and gyroscopes to process information needed to move it ahead safely)*

Follow-Up

- Use the full-size rover model and move it along the 60-centimeter distance in one minute. You may also want to place a rock at the stopping point as a target for the rover to move toward.
- *Optional Activity:* Give each group a snail and have them time how long it takes it to make the same trip of 60 centimeters.

© Teacher Created Materials, Inc.   37   #2381 Exploring Mars

Mars Pathfinder Mission

Design a Robot

Overview
Students will get the opportunity to create their own robots.

Background
Robots are playing important roles in our lives. There are robots used in movies, making cars, and doing dangerous missions on the bottom of the ocean or on Mars, such as *Sojourner*. This technology is advancing rapidly, and there will be many more uses for robots in the future. An excellent reference on modern use of robots is the article "Robot Revolution," which appeared in the July 1997 issue of *National Geographic*. Check the Resource section (page 78) for information on ordering back issues of this magazine.

Materials
- pictures of robots
- copy of Design a Robot (page 39) for each student
- *Optional:* toy robot
- parent letter (page 40) for each student

Preparation
Create a display of the materials and pictures on robots to awaken student interest.

Procedure and Discussion
1. Tell the students that the *Sojourner* rover on Mars is actually a robot, controlled by scientists on Earth, 119 million miles away. It can roam the surface of Mars without all the equipment a human would need to survive on that planet.
2. Discuss the display items and ask students where they have seen robots being used.
3. Divide the students into small groups and let them discuss what robots they would like to see invented.
4. Distribute the data sheet Design a Robot and have students complete it.

Follow-Up
- Tell the students that they are to design and construct a robot at home, using simple and inexpensive materials.
- Set a due date for the robots to be brought to school, allowing enough time for students to really be creative.
- Distribute a parent letter to explain the homework. A sample parent letter is provided for your use. Attach the student's design of a robot to the letter before they are sent home.
- When the robots are brought to school, have each student describe what her or his robot is designed to do.
- Put the finished products on display in the room and invite parents and other classes to see them.

#2381 Exploring Mars   38   © *Teacher Created Materials, Inc.*

Mars Pathfinder Mission

Design a Robot *(cont.)*

To the Students: Robots are used to do dangerous work, like that done by the *Sojourner* rover on Mars. They are also used in many movies. The dinosaurs in *Jurassic Park* are a good example. Some robots are even designed to build cars or play games like ping pong.

Don't you wish you had a special robot of your own? Now is your chance to create a picture of your robot, showing what it looks like and explaining what it does.

My Special Robot

When you finish your drawing, add labels to the parts of your robot to explain what it does.

My special robot's name is

© *Teacher Created Materials, Inc.*   39   *#2381 Exploring Mars*

Mars Pathfinder Mission

Design a Robot *(cont.)*

Sample Parent Letter

Dear Parents:

We are studying the Mars *Pathfinder* mission that landed on Mars July 4, 1997. It had a very special robot rover on board named *Sojourner*, which means "visitor." Ask your child what he or she has learned about this small but important robot. It was sent to Mars to test the soil and rocks as it roams about a football field-sized area near the Mars *Pathfinder* Lander.

The class has discussed other types of robots. This was followed by each student designing his or her own personal robot. Have your child show you the robot design made in class. Ask him or her to explain what that special robot does.

Each student was asked to design and build a robot at home. You are welcome to help your child, but the robot should be mostly of the student's own design and construction. It doesn't have to be fancy or even capable of moving, but it does need to be designed to do something.

Ask your child to explain what the robot is supposed to do.

Use simple inexpensive materials such as those listed below:

- foil
- cardboard tubes
- wooden sticks
- old clothing

- shoebox
- Styrofoam
- lids
- plastic containers

This project should be completed by _____ so your child can bring the robot to class to show it to us and tell all about it. Every student's robot will be on display in our classroom. We plan to invite other classes to come to see them. You are also welcome to visit the class to see these great robots.

Thanks for helping your child create his or her very own robot.

Sincerely,

#2381 Exploring Mars   40   © *Teacher Created Materials, Inc.*

Mars Pathfinder Mission

3-D View of Mars

Overview

Students will use special viewers to simulate the three-dimensional view seen by the scientist in charge of the rover.

Background

After landing, the rover was controlled by Brian Cooper from Jet Propulsion Laboratory (JPL) in Pasadena, California. He used special 3-D goggles and images sent from the lander's camera to see where the rover was. He moved a rover-shaped cursor on his computer to move *Sojourner* along the surface of Mars. The rover was sent to rocks JPL scientists wanted *Sojourner* to examine. The computer calculated how the rover should get to the rock and sent the message to the lander, which sent it on to *Sojourner.* It took 11 minutes for the commands to travel from Earth to Mars.

The three-dimensional views came from the two stereoscopic cameras mounted on the *Sojourner* rover with information relayed back to Earth via the lander. The stereoscopic color-camera Imager on Mars *Pathfinder* (IMP) lander sent 3-D colored images to Earth by using three filters (red, green, and blue) to send identical images that, when merged, showed the colors.

Materials

- pattern for 3-D goggles
- tagboard
- red and blue filters (plastic theme covers or filters)
- scissors
- tape
- *3-D images

*See Resources (page 79) for Web site address for 3-D images available from JPL. The cover and cover story in the July 4, 1997, issue of *Time* show pictures of the rover which are 3-D when viewed with glasses with red and blue filters.

Preparation

- Follow the instructions on page 42 to create 3-D glasses.
- Contact *Time* magazine (800) 843-TIME to order the July 14, 1997, issue. Other options: contact parents or a public library to get this issue.

Procedure

1. Post the 3-D pictures on a bulletin board in strong light. (The lenses tend to filter out light and make the picture dimmer.)
2. Have students hold glasses so the red is in front of the left eye. The 3-D images should be viewed from several distances. Usually more depth is visible from a greater distance.
3. View the image(s) without glasses to see the red and blue dots.

For Discussion

- Discuss how these images are created when the red/blue glasses are combined with the stereoscopic view of two eyes. (*Each eye is bringing in the image it sees through the red or blue filter, and the combination creates the three-dimensional effect.*)
- Have the students look at the pictures from *Time* magazine and discuss which area they would program the rover to visit and why.

© *Teacher Created Materials, Inc.*   *41*   *#2381 Exploring Mars*

Mars Pathfinder Mission

3-D View of Mars *(cont.)*

Making 3-D glasses

Instructions:

- Trace the pattern on tagboard or light cardboard.
- Cut out the holes for the filters.
- Tape a piece of red filter over one eye opening and blue over the other. Be sure they match up with the information written on the frames so the red will be in front of the left eye.
- Fold the glasses together with the filters between. Tape or staple the edges.

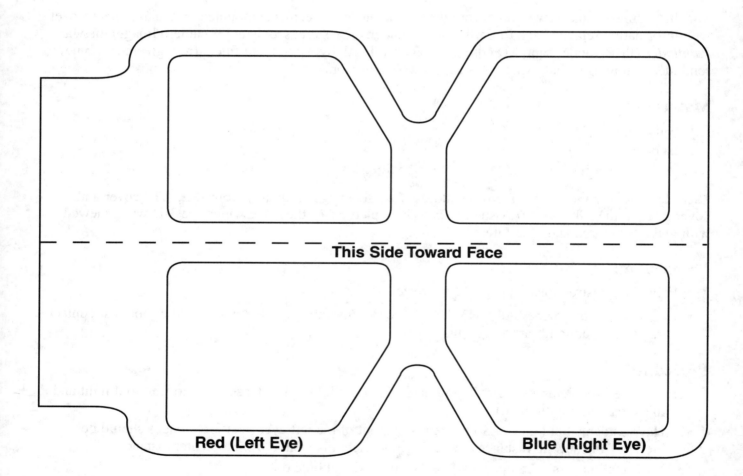

#2381 Exploring Mars 42 © Teacher Created Materials, Inc.

Mars Pathfinder Mission

Incoming Command

Overview

Students will experience a simulation of sending a message to Mars with an 11-minute delay.

Background

Messages sent into space travel at the speed of light (around 186,000 mps). Commands sent from JPL to the *Sojourner,* or to JPL from the lander, travel 119 million miles. This means the time it takes the messages to reach their respective destinations is about 11 minutes. The calculations for this follow:

119,000,000 miles ÷ 186,000 mps = 639.78 seconds (640 seconds)

640 seconds ÷ 60 seconds = 10.66 minutes (11 minutes)

On Sol 6, *Sojourner* headed for a bear-shaped rock named Yogi, swiveling its wheels and pushing sideways into position to climb the rock. Unfortunately, a small piece of rock stuck out at the base where *Sojourner* tried to climb. As one of the wheels began to roll up the rock's side, the sensors detected a tilt and shut the rover down so it would not tip over. This left the rover hanging on the rock, with two of its six wheels off the ground, creating the first motor-vehicle accident on Mars.

Scientists tried to restart *Sojourner* to back off the rock but with no luck. The rover's messages are relayed to and from Earth through the lander. The lander is shut down each Martian night when its solar batteries no longer work. Since the *Pathfinder* scientists had not reawakened the lander, there was no time before sunset on Mars to send a message that day. Finally, late the next afternoon, a scientist shouted "Flight Control, we have rover data." The rover was back in the game and backed off Yogi. Later, it was commanded to investigate rocks called Scooby Doo and Casper.

Materials

- transparency of Delta II Rocket (page 45)
- transparency of the Mars *Pathfinder* lander (page 46)
- model of the *Sojourner* rover made in Build Your Own Microrover
- Mars *Pathfinder* Lander Information (pages 35 and 46)
- copies of Mars *Pathfinder* Lander cutout model (pages 47 and 48)
- scissors
- clear tape
- glue
- blue pens or crayons
- minute timer
- rock about the size of a football

Preparation

- Make transparencies of the Mars *Pathfinder* Lander and Delta II rocket pictures. Use a transparency pen or felt pen to color the petals and top of the rover blue, representing solar panels.

- Copy Mars *Pathfinder* Lander cutout model on tagboard or heavy paper for each student.

- Locate a site (a large wall) to project the lander image to its full nine-foot (3 m) diameter. Conduct this activity at that location.

© *Teacher Created Materials, Inc.*   43   *#2381 Exploring Mars*

Mars Pathfinder Mission

Incoming Command *(cont.)*

Procedure

1. Show the transparency of the Delta II rocket and share the information about it.

2. Project the transparency of the Mars *Pathfinder* Lander on the wall so it is actual size and the bottom of the picture is at floor level.

3. Place the rover model so that it is on the floor in front of the rover in the picture. Put the large rock about two feet (61 cm) from the rover.

4. Use the Mars *Pathfinder* Lander information to help describe it.

5. Explain to the students that when they listen to the radio, it takes time for the sound to travel from the broadcasting studio to their radio. This sound is traveling at the speed of light, and they are close to the station so they hear the sound almost immediately.

6. Tell them that commands sent from Earth to the Mars *Pathfinder* landing site on Mars are sent out from the Jet Propulsion Laboratory (JPL) in Pasadena, California, and also travel at the speed of light. Earth and Mars were 119 million miles apart when the rover was roaming around on Mars. It took 11 minutes for their commands to travel all the way from Earth to Mars, and 11 minutes for scientists to receive information sent back to Earth from Mars.

7. Explain that they are going to pretend that a message has just been sent by scientists on Earth to the rover on Mars.

8. Tell them they are going to do a project while waiting the 11 minutes it takes for the message to get to Mars. (Set the timer for 11 minutes.)

   • Distribute a copy of the Mars *Pathfinder* Lander cutout model to each student, along with scissors, tape, and glue.

   • Go over the instructions with the students.

9. When the timer goes off, stop working on the models and tell the students the message has arrived at Mars. The rover has been told to move off the petal of the lander and drive to the rock. Ask one of the students to move the model rover away from the lander petal and toward the rock. Have the students give the rock a name.

10. Tell them that the rover moves so slowly it will take time for it to get to the rock. Explain that they can continue to build their models while the rover moves toward the rock.

For Discussion

Discuss how this slow communication might affect the progress of the rover on Mars. Example: The *Sojourner* was commanded to move toward a bear-shaped rock named Yogi on Sol 5 (its fifth day on Mars). It got a little excited and began to climb the rock. As one of its wheels began rolling up the side of Yogi, sensors on board thought it might tip over and shut down the rover motors. It was hung up on the side of the rock until the scientists on Earth could send a message to start the rover again and get it to back off. One of the scientists declared that "This was the first motor vehicle accident on Mars."

#2381 Exploring Mars   44   © *Teacher Created Materials, Inc.*

Mars Pathfinder Mission

Incoming Command (cont.)

Mars *Pathfinder's* Launch Vehicle: Delta II Rocket

The Mars *Pathfinder* Lander was carried at the top of the Delta II rocket launched from Cape Canaveral on December 4, 1996. Three stages of rockets fired, one after the other, with each falling away after it was no longer needed. Finally, the spacecraft was on a 310 million-mile path that took it through space. It landed on Mars seven months later on July 4, 1997.

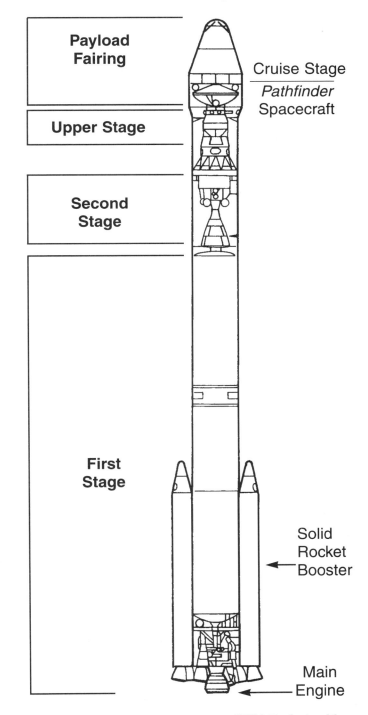

After Lift Off
5 minutes

Payload Fairing
Fairing (cover) over payload opens and falls away. Altitude: 81 miles (130 km)

After Lift Off
70 minutes
73 minutes

Upper Stage
Upper stage fires and then separates from spacecraft.

After Lift Off
4.5 minutes

Second Stage
Second-stage engine fires as the first stage falls away. Altitude: 79 miles (126 km)

69 minutes

Second Stage falls away.

Lift Off

First Stage
First stage engine and six of its nine booster rockets ignite.

1 minute

Six boosters are ejected, falling back into the ocean.

2 minutes

Last three boosters are fired. Last boosters are ejected. Altitude: 34 miles (54 km)

© Teacher Created Materials, Inc. 45 #2381 Exploring Mars

Mars Pathfinder Mission

Incoming Command (cont.)

Mars *Pathfinder* Lander

The Mars *Pathfinder* Lander arrived at Mars on July 6, 1997, after launching aboard a Delta II rocket from Cape Canaveral on December 4, 1996. This lander looked like a small pyramid standing about three feet (.9 m) high when folded up. It consisted of three triangular petals, each about three feet (.9 m) long, attached to a six-sided base. Within this spacecraft were packed the small *Sojourner* rover and the command center which would gather data from the rover to relay to Earth. It would also collect images of the landing area and information on the weather and magnetic field. The lander's three petals are covered with solar panels, each 35.5 square feet (3.3 square meters) to supply energy during the day. At night, the lander will operate on rechargeable batteries.

The lander was surrounded by heavy-duty air bags that inflated just before it hit the Martian surface. It bounced 50 feet (15 m) high on first contact, with the next 15 bounces bringing it lower, until it finally stopped. When the lander first opened, one of the air bags did not fully deflate. This blocked the ramp which would let *Sojourner* roll off the landing platform to explore the planet. The scientists were able to send a command to the lander to finish deflating the air bag just before losing contact with the planet as it rotated away from Earth. The next morning, they were able to get the rover to roll down the ramp, and it began exploring. "Six wheels on soil!" exclaimed one JPL scientist. This was like Astronaut Neil Armstrong's statement, "One small step for mankind," as he stepped on the moon 28 years ago.

The lander was renamed the *Sagan Memorial Station,* in honor of Dr. Carl Sagan, a well-known astronomer who had been one of the leaders in exploration of Mars by satellites and landers. Dr. Sagan died in 1997 before the landing of the Mars *Pathfinder*.

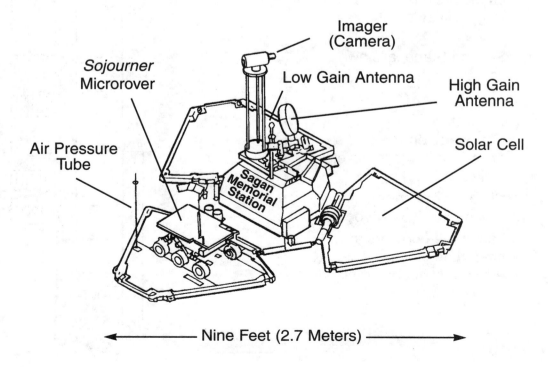

#2381 Exploring Mars   46   © Teacher Created Materials, Inc.

Mars *Pathfinder* Mission

Incoming Command *(cont.)*

Mars *Pathfinder* Lander

Scale: 1/17th

(This cutout model is a modified version of that created by Jet Propulsion Laboratory at California Institute of Technology. Printed by permission of JPL/California Institute of Technology, Pasadena, California.)

Instructions: Cut out the station and microrover. Color the solar panel on the top of the microrover blue. Fold along the dotted lines on each model, bending these parts under the top. Use clear tape to hold the tabs under the sides to form boxes.

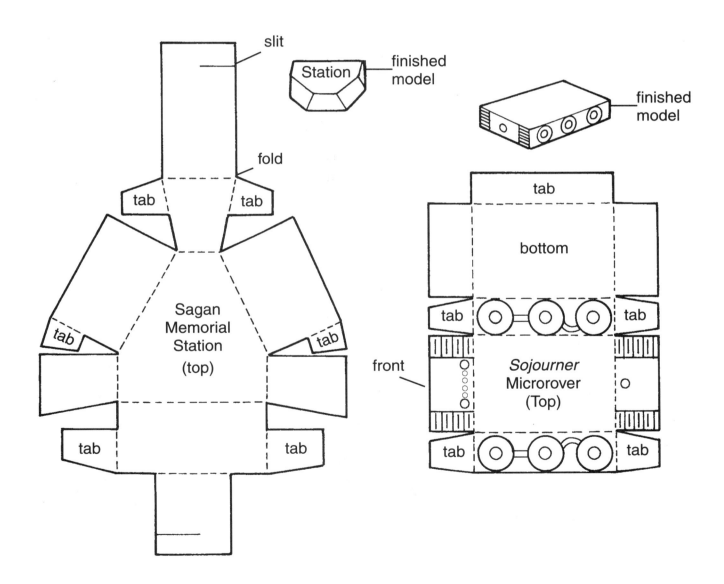

© Teacher Created Materials, Inc.　　　47　　　#2381 Exploring Mars

Mars Pathfinder Mission

Incoming Command (cont.)

Mars *Pathfinder* Lander

Instructions: Cut out the lander, carefully cutting the slits as marked. Color the solar panels blue on the three triangular petals of the lander. Fold upward along the dotted lines on each of the petals. Glue the electronics box and microrover on to the lander base where shown.

Fold up the three petals and place the slit of each tab in the slit at the top edge of the next petal. This will show the lander in its position just before landing and opening its petals.

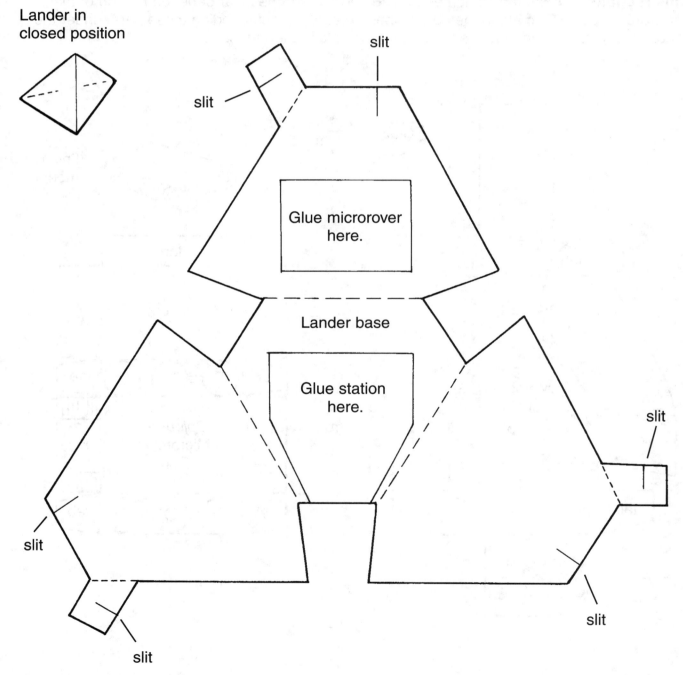

#2381 Exploring Mars   48   © Teacher Created Materials, Inc.

Mars Pathfinder Mission

The Little Rover That Could

Overview
Students will learn about the trip of the Mars *Pathfinder* from Earth to Mars.

Background
The Mars *Pathfinder* was launched aboard a Delta II rocket from Cape Canaveral on December 4, 1996. It traveled 310 million miles from Earth to Mars, landing about 10:00 A.M. Pacific Time on July 4, 1997, on Mars in the area known as Ares Vallis.

This story depicts the details of the Mars *Pathfinder's* trip to Mars, as told by the *Sojourner* rover. Illustrations for the story are included to show to students as the story unfolds.

Materials
- copy of *The Little Engine That Could* by Watty Piper, Platt & Munk Publishers, 1976
- transparency copies of illustrations (pages 51–58)
- colored transparency pens or permanent ink felt pens
- copy of the story (pages 59–62)
- color wheel instructions (page 50)
- JPL/NASA pictures about the Mars *Pathfinder* mission (see Resources, page 78)

Preparation
- Copy the story pictures on transparencies. Cut them out and then color or assemble them as directed.
- Sort the pictures in the numerical order to be shown as indicated in the story.
- Photographs of the Mars *Pathfinder* mission can be displayed in the room for additional information. (See Resources, page 78, for JPL address to order current lithographs of the mission.)
- Construct a color wheel to be used for special effects.
- If capable, students may assist in operating the scenery and color wheel for this story. At least three students will be needed for this task.

Procedure
1. Briefly discuss some of the information about *Sojourner* studied earlier.
2. Show the *Sojourner* model constructed in the activity Build Your Own Microrover.
3. Set up the overhead projector and gather the students around it.
4. Read aloud *The Little Engine That Could* and then tell the students that they are about to hear another story about a brave little rover that went to Mars.

As the story is read, place the related illustrations on the overhead projector.

For Discussion
Talk about how it would feel to be aboard the Mars *Pathfinder* mission with the little rover.

Follow-Up
- Present this illustrated story for other classes.
- Visit the Web sites that describe the Mars *Pathfinder* mission. (See Resources, page 79.)

© *Teacher Created Materials, Inc.*   49   *#2381 Exploring Mars*

Mars Pathfinder Mission

The Little Rover That Could (cont.)
(Color Wheel Instructions)

To the Teacher: Adding color to the illustrations for *The Little Rover That Could* story as they are shown on the overhead projector will create a special effect that enhances the story.

Materials
- red, green, blue, and yellow cellophane or translucent plastic covers used as theme covers and found in office supply stores
- two 16-inch (41 cm) round pizza cardboards
- yard or meter stick
- single edged razor blade
- one-inch (2.5 cm) wooden dowel
- glue or glue gun
- nail about two inches (5 cm) long

Preparation
Cut pie-shaped holes in the pizza cardboards as windows for the colored plastic filters. Have the divisions between the windows be at least 1/2 inch (1 cm) wide. The outside of the circle should be 1 inch (2.5 cm) wide.

Leave a circle of 1 1/2 inches (4 cm) in the center of the circle.

Use the cutout cardboard window as a template to trace on the color filters, using black felt pen. Leave about 1/2 inch (1.3 cm) edge when cutting the filter so it can be glued on the cardboard frame.

Glue the filters to the windows of one cardboard. Hold the wheel up to the projector light to check for color intensity. If the color is too light, add another layer of the filter.

Glue the two cardboards together with the filters sandwiched between.

Drill a hole in the center circle and put a nail through the hole and into the end of the dowel. There should be enough freedom of movement to be able to spin the color wheel slow or fast.

Color Wheel

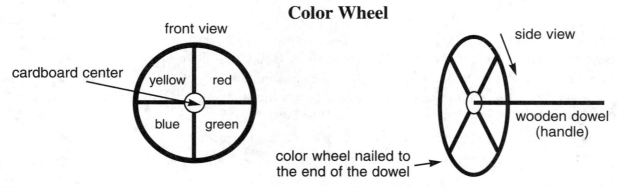

Procedure
1. Hold the handle (dowel) alongside the overhead projector so the light will shine through the colored filters. Adjust the distance so the light will not be cut off by the cardboard frame.
2. As the story is read, follow the instructions for how to use the colors.

Mars Pathfinder Mission

The Little Rover That Could *(cont.)*

Story Illustrations

To the Teacher: The pictures provided for this story should be reproduced as transparencies to be used as the story is read. A number appears beside the picture title that corresponds to the story. When cutting out the transparency of the picture, remove teacher instructions and numbers. Add a small self-adhesive label to each picture. Write the number of the picture on the label to keep them in order as you read the story. You may color the pictures with overhead transparency or permanent ink felt pens to enhance them if you like (e.g., color the oceans blue in this picture).

#1 Earth

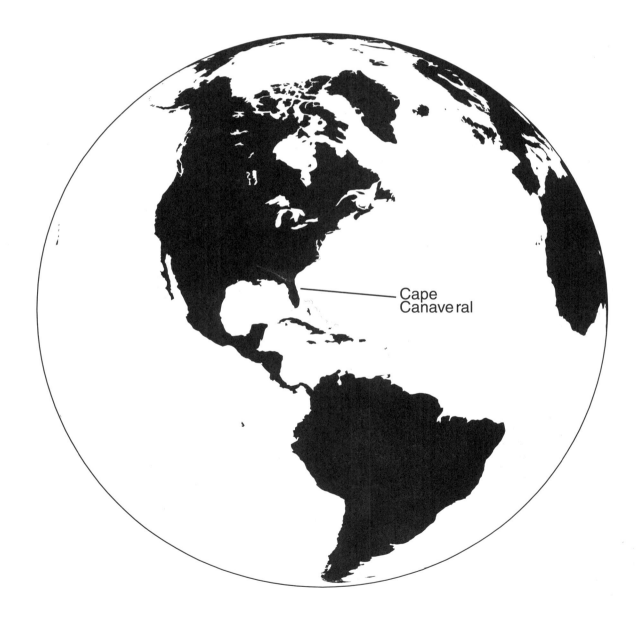

Mars Pathfinder Mission

The Little Rover That Could (cont.)

Story Illustrations (cont.)

#2 Delta II Rocket

To the Teacher: Make a transparency of this page; then use a blank transparency and use restickable glue to attach the pieces of the rocket on a clear transparency so they are fully assembled. See page 45 for a drawing of the fully assembled Delta II rocket which carried the *Pathfinder* into space. The rocket stages will be removed as the story is read.

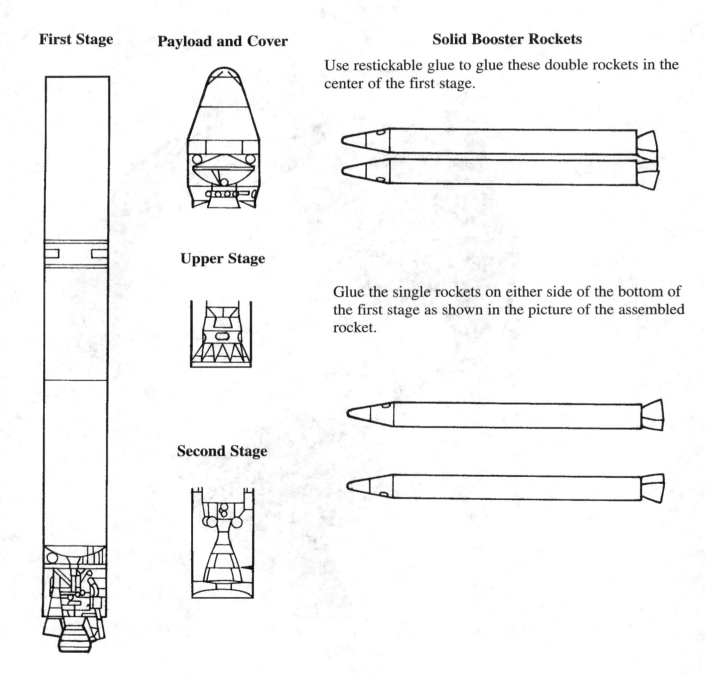

First Stage

Payload and Cover

Upper Stage

Second Stage

Solid Booster Rockets

Use restickable glue to glue these double rockets in the center of the first stage.

Glue the single rockets on either side of the bottom of the first stage as shown in the picture of the assembled rocket.

#2381 Exploring Mars © Teacher Created Materials, Inc.

Mars Pathfinder Mission

The Little Rover That Could *(cont.)*

Story Illustrations *(cont.)*

#3 Earth-to-Mars Route

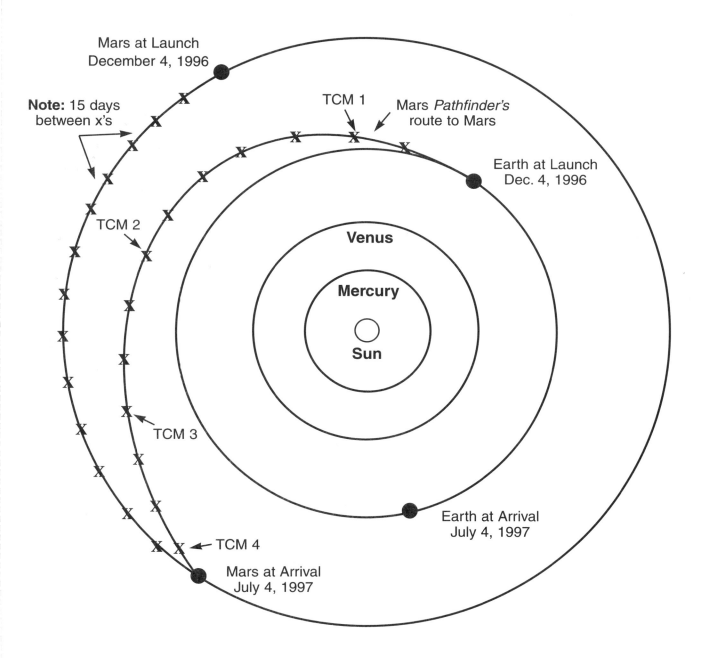

TCM = Trajectory Correction Maneuver, when the boosters fire to adjust the course of the *Pathfinder*.

Mars Pathfinder Mission

The Little Rover That Could (cont.)

Story Illustrations (cont.)
#4 Mars Landing Site

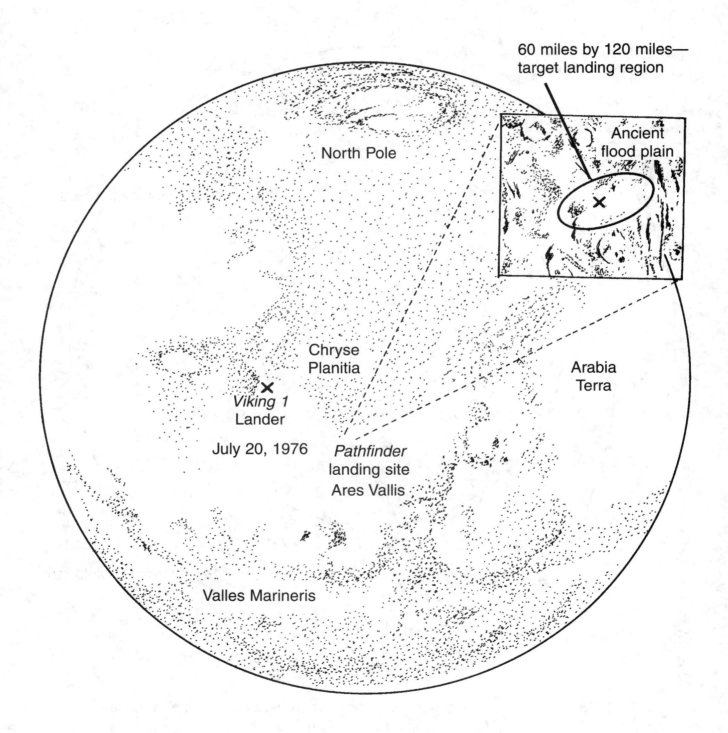

#2381 Exploring Mars

The Little Rover That Could (cont.)

Story Illustrations (cont.)

#5 Cruise Stage

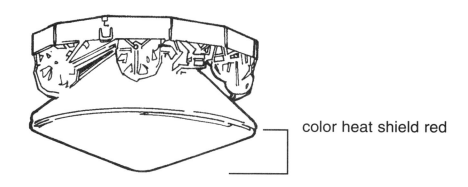

color heat shield red

#6 Mars *Pathfinder* Lander

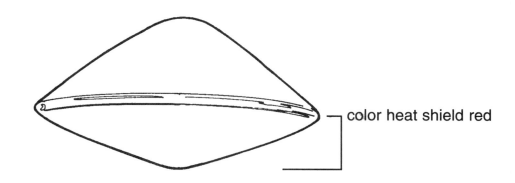

color heat shield red

Mars Pathfinder Mission

The Little Rover That Could (cont.)

Story Illustrations (cont.)

#7A Mars Landing Sequence

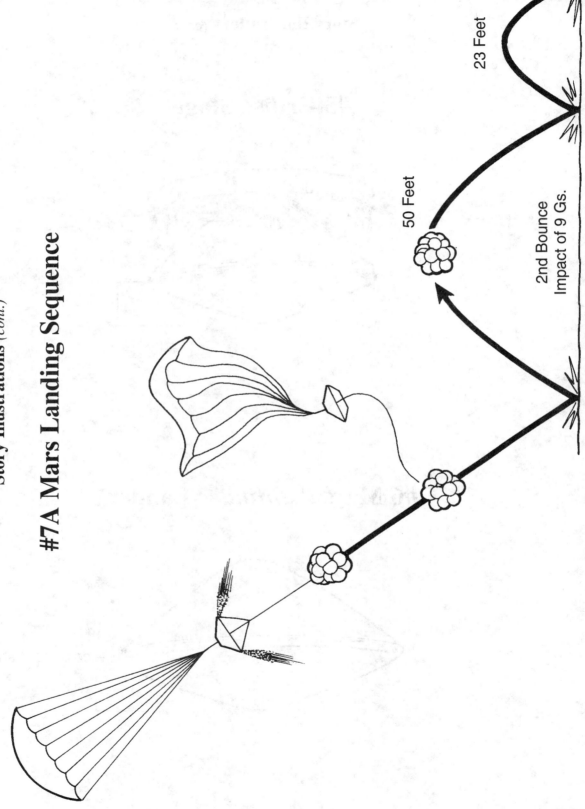

#2381 Exploring Mars — 56 — © Teacher Created Materials, Inc.

The Little Rover That Could *(cont.)*

Story Illustrations *(cont.)*

#7B Mars Landing Sequence *(cont.)*

To the Teacher: Link this picture to the previous page to make the continuous landing sequence. Color the sky pink around the lander and the dirt red. Color the solar panels on the lander (3) and rover blue.

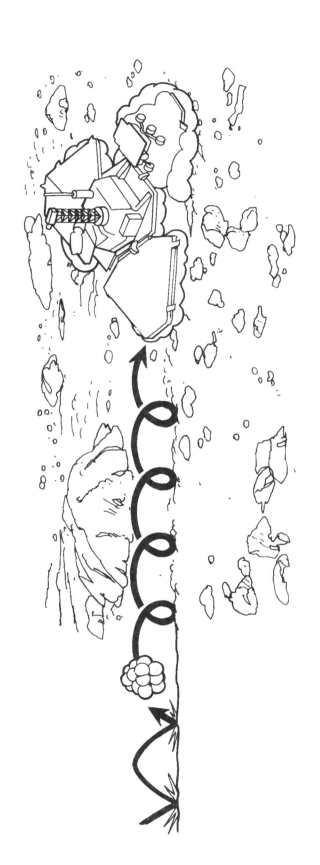

Mars Pathfinder Mission

The Little Rover That Could (cont.)

Story Illustrations (cont.)
#8 Final Picture

I knew I could,
I knew I could,
I knew I could . . .

Make it all the way to Mars!

Mars Pathfinder Mission

The Little Rover That Could *(cont.)*

(Overhead Transparency Story)

Introduction: *(Place picture #1, the Earth, on the overhead projector and point to Cape Canaveral.)* There is a lot of excitement at Cape Canaveral, Florida, today, December 4, 1996. Scientists are about to launch a Delta II rocket that will lift the Mars *Pathfinder* spacecraft off the Earth and send it on a 310-million-mile journey to the planet Mars. Inside the spacecraft is a vehicle no bigger than a small microwave oven. It is called the *Sojourner* Mars Rover, and it will have a big job to do when it reaches Mars. Let's listen to the rover's story and follow along on its trip to Mars.

(Place picture #2, the rocket, on the overhead projector.)

Hello, I'm *Sojourner*, which means "visitor." That's a good name for me since I am about to make a VERY long trip to visit another planet. I'm sitting inside this giant rocket, getting ready to launch off the Earth. If you look really hard, you might be able to see inside the rocket. Look way up at the top to see the *Pathfinder* Spacecraft.

(Point to Mars Pathfinder *Spacecraft near top of rocket.)*

I'm inside and near the bottom of this spacecraft. It is really tightly packed in here. I am squashed in a box shaped like a closed up flower with a flat bottom and a triangular-shaped petal attached to each side. I have six wheels which are pushed up under me to save space. I am crammed against the other pieces of equipment going on this trip with me. There is a special camera to take 3-D pictures of Mars' surface and instruments that will measure the weather conditions. All this important information will be sent back to scientists on Earth. It will take 11 minutes to reach them since Mars and Earth will be 119 million miles apart.

I can hear the countdown now to light the six solid boosters and the first-stage engine. Oh no! It must be time to launch!

(Place the red filter in front of the light, and then spin the color wheel fast at the blast off.)

5, 4, 3, 2, 1, BLAST OFF! OH, WHAT A NOISE! I didn't think it would be this noisy or shake so much. I don't think I want to go anymore. But I have a very important job to do. All the scientists that worked to build me are counting on me to tell them what Mars is like.

I think I can, I think I can, I think I can last through the blast.

(Continue spinning color wheel. Remove center boosters.)

What's that terrible noise? It must be the second set of solid booster rockets firing. The other boosters have run out of fuel and quit firing. They will fall into the ocean on Earth.

(Continue spinning color wheel. Remove outer boosters and then remove first stage.)

There go the other boosters falling off into the ocean. We are now 33 miles (57 km) above the Earth, and it only took about two minutes to get this high. Oh no! The main engine has shut down—it is sooo quiet now! We are still traveling very fast, and we are 73 miles (118 km) above the Earth.

© *Teacher Created Materials, Inc.*   *#2381 Exploring Mars*

Mars Pathfinder Mission

The Little Rover That Could *(cont.)*

(Overhead Transparency Story) *(cont.)*

(Place the red filter in front of the light, and then spin the color wheel fast.)

WOW! Another blast . . . that must be the second stage firing. Shhhh! It just got quiet again. The second stage engine must have turned off. We have been flying for only nine minutes, and already we are 117 miles (189 km) above Earth. If I had a window, I could see all the state of Florida. It is sooo quiet again!

I think I can, I think I can, I think I can live through the silence.

(Place the red filter in front of the light, and then spin the color wheel slowly.)

We have been coasting for almost an hour. I am feeling a little dizzy since we have been slowly rolling to get into the right position to go to Mars. This is called the "barbecue roll maneuver." I sure hope I don't get sick.

(Place the red filter in front of the light, and then spin the color wheel fast.)

There it goes again! Another blast of the second stage rocket. I hate that roar! I'm going to be deaf before this is over.

I think I can, I think I can, I think I can last through the blast.

(Remove second stage rocket)

Ah! Silence at last! The second stage is falling away, and we are on a path that will take us from Earth to Mars.

I think I can, I think I can, I think I can last through the silence.

(Place the red filter in front of the light, and then spin the color wheel fast.)

Well, it was 70 minutes ago that we launched, and it's about time for the last engine blast.
Get ready . . . 5, 4, 3, 2, 1, BLAST OFF!

I think I can, I think I can, I think I can last through the blast.

(Show upper stage falling away. Slowly spin the color wheel.)

YAHOO! The upper stage has separated and the spinning has slowed down. I am so glad to have it quiet again. I think I'll try to get some sleep; this is going to be a LONG trip.

I thought I could, I thought I could, I thought I could *(sigh)* last through the blasts.

— Pause —

(Picture #3 of Earth-Mars route map)

It has been 30 days since we left Earth. This map shows where we are now—still a long way to go. It has been nice and quiet in here.

(Place the red filter in front of the light and then spin the color wheel fast.)

What was that? Oh no, not ANOTHER BLAST!

I think I can, I think I can, I think I can last through another blast.

#2381 Exploring Mars 60 © *Teacher Created Materials, Inc.*

Mars Pathfinder Mission

The Little Rover That Could *(cont.)*

(Overhead Transparency Story) *(cont.)*

(Point to TCM #1 on map. Stop spinning of color wheel.)

At least that one was not as long. It must have been the four small thruster engines firing to put us on the right course towards Mars. There will be more of these short blasts to make sure we don't miss Mars. I hope they work! It would be terrible to go through all of this and zip past Mars and into outer space. I really want to land so I can roam around Ares Vallis on Mars.

— Pause —

(Point to TCM #4. Slowly spin the color wheel.)

We are only 15 days from Mars. Everything is OK. I've been able to get some rest, even though we have been spinning. It's like being on a slow merry-go-round.

I think I will, I think I will, I think I will be OK.

(Picture #4, Mars from a distance. Use the red filter.)

I can't believe it has been seven months since we blasted off from Earth. It's July 3, and we have only 12 hours until we land on Mars. That will be right on schedule—July 4th, Independence Day for the United States. What a fantastic way to celebrate that holiday! Of course, I wouldn't get to see any fireworks way out here, but that's OK. I will be having a thrilling ride at touchdown time! I have to get ready for landing.

I think I can, I think I can, I think I can live through the landing.

(Show picture #5 cruise stage.)

It's 37 minutes to landing on Mars which is still 8,000 miles (5,000 km) away. We are about to separate from the cruise stage.

(Picture #5 Use red filter. Spin the color wheel.)

Oh, oh! It is heating up in here! I sure hope that heat shield works so we don't melt going through the atmosphere of Mars. Our speed is 17,500 miles per hour. I feel like I am being squashed because of the increased gravity caused by our fast falling toward Mars. Five minutes to landing and 80 miles (50 km) to go!

I think I can, I think I can, I think I can survive the heat and pressure.

(Show picture #6 of red hot lander closed up.)

Time for me to get ready for my grand arrival on Mars. I know everyone back on Earth is as excited about this event as I am. The cruise stage just dropped the lander. If everything goes as planned, the 36-foot (12-meters) parachute should open next to slow the lander down. It had better work!

(Show picture #7, landing sequence, exposing it gradually to follow the story. Slowly turn color wheel.)

(Scream!) What was that noise and that sudden jerk? It must have been the parachute being shot out to slow our fall. At last! Now, we are floating, thanks to the parachute, but still falling. It is a much slower fall, so the pressure is a lot less. I feel like I just lost a lot of weight. That noise must be the air bags inflating. So far, so good!

© *Teacher Created Materials, Inc.*   *#2381 Exploring Mars*

Mars Pathfinder Mission

The Little Rover That Could *(cont.)*

(Overhead Transparency Story) *(cont.)*

We will hit the surface of Mars, bouncing like a huge ball on the air bags surrounding the lander. Let's hope the air bags hold up. If not, I will end up as flat as a piece of paper.

Another blast, this time it is the parachute dropping the lander and its air bags.

I think I can, I think I can, I think I can live through the landing.

(Picture #7, lander bouncing 50 feet)

Oh! Oh! Oh! I'm bouncing! That first bounce must have been 50 feet high, and the last one wasn't much better—probably 23 feet high. Twelve, thirteen, fourteen, fifteen, SIXTEEN BOUNCES! Wow! We have finally stopped bouncing. WE ARE ON MARS!

I thought I could, I thought I could, I thought I could live through the landing!

(Picture #7 lander petals open. Mars showing pink sky and red soil.)

Now, the petals of the lander are opening up. Oh what a beautiful sight! The sky is PINK and the dirt is RED! We sure aren't on Earth anymore! There are rocks everywhere and nothing growing. It looks like the Arizona desert back home, but I don't see any cactus or coyotes.

There is a problem with the air bags, however. One of them is still slightly inflated. I can't get down the ramp of the lander to begin roaming around Mars until it is deflated. We'll have to wait for the scientists back at JPL to do something about that. It takes 11 minutes for the command message to reach us here on Mars. I think it will be morning before I can roam around sniffing the rocks and taking pictures to be sent back to Earth.

(Picture #8, Sign "I Knew I Could . . . .)

I knew I could,

I knew I could,

I knew I could . . .

make it all the way to Mars!

The Martians Have Landed!

Launching to Mars

Overview
Students will walk out the orbits of Mars and Earth to simulate a launch from Earth to Mars.

Background

Mars is farther from the sun than Earth and therefore takes more time to make its yearly journey. The distance between the two planets is constantly changing. There are times when they will be closer together—the best times to plan to launch a vehicle from Earth to Mars. The orbit of Mars is well known by scientists who can predict the best years to launch spacecraft to Mars.

Any spacecraft launched from Earth to Mars must follow a curved path to cross the vast distances between the planets. During that time, Mars will have moved in its orbit. Therefore, the spacecraft must be aimed toward the location where Mars will be when it reaches its orbit. Minor adjustments were made in the path of the Mars *Pathfinder* while it was en route to Mars. This was done by using small retrorockets fired at preprogrammed intervals during the trip to keep the craft on a path that enabled it to reach Mars.

When the Mars *Pathfinder* was launched in December 4, 1996, it took only seven months for it to reach Mars on July 4, 1997. However, Mars *Global Surveyor* was launched on November 11, 1996, but will not reach Mars until September 1997, taking 10 months. This is due to the difference in the relative distances between Mars and Earth on November 11 and December 4.

Materials
- paved area such as the playground
- chalk
- string
- tennis ball or other soft ball
- transparency of Orbits of the Inner Planets (page 11)
- transparency of Earth-Mars Orbit: 1984–2003 (page 65)

Preparation
- Draw chalk circles on pavement to represent the orbits of Mars and Earth. Tie a loop in the end of the string to hold the chalk and cut it to a length of four feet (1 m 40 cm).
- Repeat this with another string cut to six feet (2 m).
- Use the chalk to place an X in the center of the area where the circles are to be drawn. Have someone hold one end of the string on the X. Stretch out the shorter string (Earth's orbit).
- Place the chalk in the loop and draw a circle around the X (sun's position).
- Repeat this with the longer string, moving the center of the circle for Mars' orbit about six inches (15 cm) from the center of Earth's orbit.

Procedure
1. Use the Orbits of the Inner Planets transparency to review the position of Mars and Earth as they orbit the sun. Ask where Mars and Earth would need to be if we wanted to make the shortest trip to Mars.

© *Teacher Created Materials, Inc.*   63   *#2381 Exploring Mars*

The Martians Have Landed!

Launching to Mars *(cont.)*

Procedure *(cont.)*

2. Have students use the flipbooks made in Race of the Planets (pages 9–13) to review the constantly changing positions of Mars and Earth.

3. Tell the students the background information and let them know they will be doing an activity which will show why they need to plan ahead if they are to launch a spacecraft from Earth and arrive at Mars when the two planets are going to be close together.

4. Move to the playground area where the circles have been drawn.

5. Select three students: one stands on the X to represent the sun's position, another stands on Earth's orbit, and the third on Mars' orbit at the closest point to Earth.

6. Have remaining students form a large circle about two feet from Mars' orbit to observe the activity and be ready to tell about what they observed when it is over.

7. Give the ball to the "Earth" to "launch" this spacecraft to "Mars." Mars should throw the spacecraft to Earth, simulating a return of the spacecraft. Let the two planets practice tossing the spacecraft back and forth until they do it with ease.

8. Now, the two students practice walking their orbits, with Earth completing its orbit in half the time of Mars. After this practice, have them repeat the ball-tossing as they walk the orbit.

Alternate Procedure

1. If a merry-go-round is available, use it to represent the orbit of Earth. Use the footpath created by the feet of people pushing it as the orbit of Mars. Have one student represent Earth and stand on the outer edge of the merry-go-round, while another is Mars and stands on the outer circle.

2. They should practice tossing the ball back-and-forth until it is easy to do.

3. Rotate the merry-go-round at a speed which will return it to its starting point when Mars has walked only half way around.

4. Have Mars and Earth launch the spacecraft between them as they are in motion.

For Discussion

Ask the students what they have discovered about launching a spacecraft to Mars. (*It must be launched on a path to be where the planet is when the spacecraft arrives at its destination. Thus, it must be sent on a curved path aimed at a point ahead of the planet at the time of launch. The planet will move during the time it takes the spacecraft to get from Earth to Mars. If calculations are made correctly, the spacecraft will reach its destination.*)

Follow-Up

- Show the transparency of dates when Mars and Earth will be closest together so students can discuss which years would be best to go to Mars. (*1999, 2001, 2003*)

- Tell the students that in 1988, Mars was only 35 million miles from Earth; in 1997 it was 119 million miles. In 2005 Mars and Earth will be as close as they were in 1988.

#2381 Exploring Mars 64 *© Teacher Created Materials, Inc.*

Launching to Mars (cont.)

Earth-Mars Orbit: 1984–2003

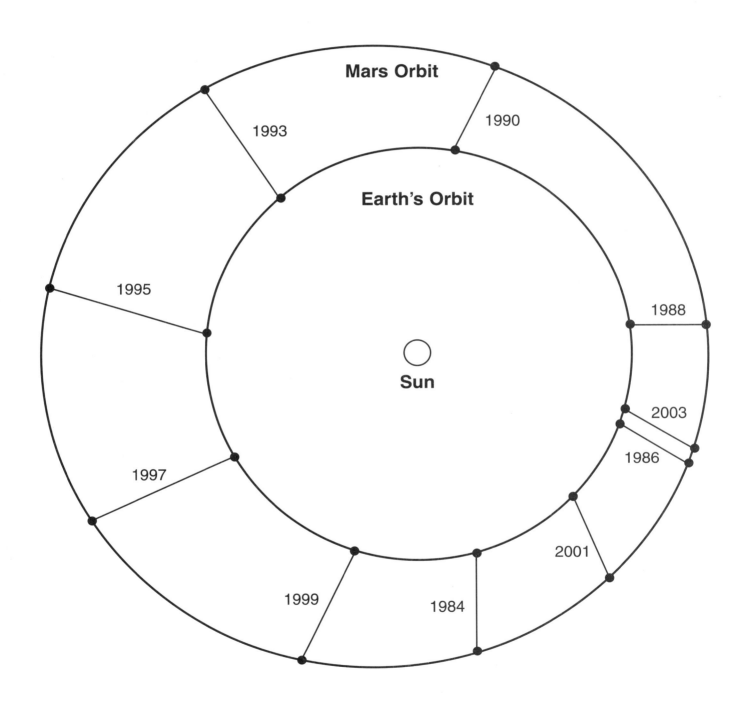

The Martians Have Landed!

Off to Mars

Overview

Students will work in teams to create an action story and scale models depicting a trip from Earth to Mars in 2011.

Background

The present cooperation between the United States, Russia, Canada, Japan, and nine European nations in the space program will likely lead to realizing the goal of placing an International Space Station (ISS) in Earth orbit. The first two parts of the ISS are scheduled to launch in late 1997. The assembly of the ISS is scheduled for 2002. When completed, the ISS will enable scientists to live aboard to conduct experiments. Ultimately, such a space station may be a launch pad for spacecraft to Mars or the moon.

Materials

- transparency of International Space Station (ISS) (page 68)
- pictures and information from JPL and NASA regarding future spacecraft designed to go to Mars (See JPL and NASA in Resources, page 78.)
- Web site information on future exploration of Mars (See Resources Web site section, page 79.)
- map of the surface of Mars (See The Planetary Society in Resources, page 78.)
- copy of "Mission to Mars" by astronaut Michael Collins. (See Resources for details, page 77.)
- copy of 1996 Mars Mission NASA Press Kit (See Resources for details, page 78.)
- videotape of JPL Computer Graphics including *Mars the Movie*
- copies of crew assignments (pages 71–75)
- wide variety of materials students can supply from home for the construction of their models

Preparation

- Read Future Mars Exploration: Teacher Background (page 70).

- Gather information and pictures of future spacecraft to be used in the exploration of Mars. This will be necessary for the students to use in their projects.

- Contact JPL (818) 354-4321 Teacher Resource Center to request information for obtaining the 100-minute video *JPL Computer Graphics*. This video contains a five-minute animation of a flyover of Mars' surface made using the data from *Vikings 1* and *2*. It begins with a representation of both planets to compare sizes and physical features. Closeups of the Martian surface showing the chain of three volcanoes and the 2,500 miles (4,000 km) long Valles Marineris are followed by a simulated flight over this area.

Procedure

1. Share the information about the ISS and scheduled future missions to Mars. Review the materials you gathered to describe future missions to Mars.

2. Display the Mars map and point out the huge volcano Olympus Mons, the chain of three volcanoes, and the huge Valles Marineris.

3. Show the video *Mars the Movie*. Repeat this five-minute section at least twice so students will be able to relate it to the Mars map and begin to "feel" what the planet looks like.

#2381 Exploring Mars 66 © *Teacher Created Materials, Inc.*

Off to Mars *(cont.)*

Procedure *(cont.)*

4. Use the Mars map to show where the landing sites of *Viking 1* and *2*. Place a marker on the map on the Mars *Pathfinder* landing site (19 degrees N, 34 degrees W). Tell the students this was just 525 miles (840 km) southwest of the *Viking 1* landing spot.

5. Divide the students into five groups and distribute their crew assignments. Assign more members to the Sagan Station group than the others. Review the assignments with each group.

6. Allow enough time for students to do their research, make their designs, and construct their models. Be sure each group knows what the others are doing so the models all tie together.

For Discussion

- Discuss the assignments with the entire class to provide them with an overview of the scale models that will be constructed.
- Be sure they understand what is expected of them and that they will need to check with the other groups as directed. For example, explain that the Space Station model will need to have docking ports that will accommodate the Earth-to-Space Station Shuttle and Mars Transporter.

Follow-Up

- When students have completed their projects, have them describe them to the class.
- Set up a display of the student's projects and have them write scripts to describe each one.
- If available, use a video camera to record the presentations of each group, in order, from the beginning launch to arriving at Mars. Include close-up pictures of each project.
- Invite other classes and parents to visit a display of the projects.
- Check Web sites for current information on the Mars *Global Surveyor* missions. It is scheduled to reach Mars in September 1997, and will begin mapping Mars' surface in March 1998.

Route of the 1996 Mars *Global Surveyor*

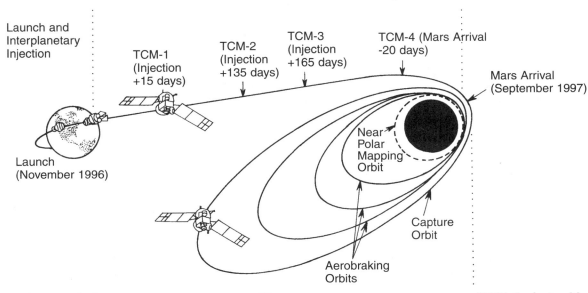

The Martians Have Landed!

Off to Mars *(cont.)*

International Space Station

Phase 2: Assembly (scheduled to begin late 1997)

(1) Functional Cargo Block (11/97)
(2) Node 1 (12/97)
(3) Service Module (4/98)
(4) Soyuz crew transfer vehicle (5/98)
(5) Universal Docking Module (6/98)
(6) Z1 (6/98)
(7) Solar power module and array (9/98)
(8) Science power platform (9/98)
(9) US Laboratory Module (11/98)
(10) Space Station Remote Manipulator System (12/98)
(11) Airlock and high pressure gas tanks (3/99)

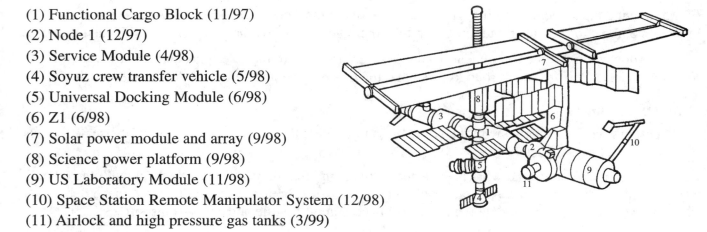

Assembly Completed (scheduled for 2002)

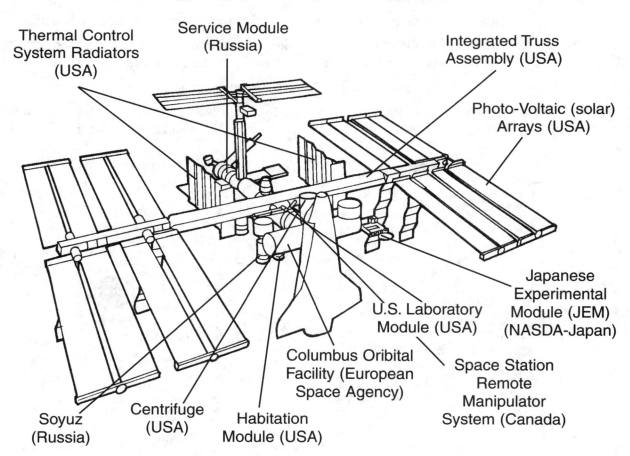

#2381 Exploring Mars © Teacher Created Materials, Inc.

The Martians Have Landed!

Off to Mars *(cont.)*

International Space Station

Facts

Wingspan end-to-end width. . . . . 361 feet (110 meters)
Length . . . . 290 feet (88.3 meters)
Mass (weight). . . . . 924,000 pounds (419,126 kilograms)
Operating distance above Earth. . . . . 220 miles average (407 kilometers)
Atmosphere inside living areas . . . . same as Earth's at sea level
14.7 pounds per square inch
(101.35 kilonewtons)
Crew size . . . . 6 people when station is fully assembled

Time Line for Completion

Date	Sections and Function
11/97	(1) Functional Cargo Block, automated spacecraft to provide control for maintaining correct orientation during orbit and propulsion during early assembly phases. Solar power and berthing ports for models to be added later. Similar to Russian *Mir* modules.
12/97	(2) Node 1 to be delivered by Space Shuttle. It will provide storage for supplies, attachment points for modules and the station's large truss and docking port for the shuttle.
4/98	(3) Service module constructed by Russia, this will be the living and working area for three crew members.
5/98	(4) Soyuz (Russian) crew transfer vehicle used when Space Shuttle is not available or in case of emergency. A three-person crew can now live on the space station.
6/98	(5) Universal Docking Module will serve as docking port for research modules, a Life Support Module and another Soyuz transfer vehicle.
	(6) ZI delivered by Space Shuttle (STS 91). The crew will attach this segment to the space station. They will also bring communication and other equipment.
9/98	(7) Solar power module and solar panels will be added by the U.S.
	(8) Science power platform will be launched by Russia. It will provide power and heat rejection for space science and operations.
11/98	(9) U.S. laboratory module will carry experiment racks, plus life support, maintenance, and control systems.
12/98	(10) Space station remote manipulator system, made by Canada, it is 55 feet (16.5 m) long and can move 125 tons of modules and equipment. This robotic system assists with assembly, spacewalks, and regular space station maintenance or repairs.
2/99	First utilization flight completes outfitting of the U.S. lab module.
3/99	(11) Airlock and high pressure gas tanks will support spacewalks. Phase 2 ends.

Assembly Completion

11/99	First Russian research module added.
3/2000	Japanese experiment module (JEM) launch.
8/2001	Centrifuge accommodation module launched by U.S.
9/2001	Columbus Ortibal Facility European Lab launched by European Space Agency (ESA).
2/2002	Habitation module launched by U.S.
6/2002	Assembly is completed, full 6-person crew can live aboard the Space Station.

The Martians Have Landed!

Off to Mars *(cont.)*

Future Mars Exploration

Teacher Background

The Mars *Pathfinder* and Mars *Global Surveyor* are two separate NASA programs. Mars *Pathfinder* is a single project under NASA's Discovery program, created in 1992 to find low-cost solar system missions.

Mars *Global Surveyor* is the first in a multi-year series of missions under the Mars *Surveyor* program. Launch of the Mars *Global Surveyor* in November 1996 kicked off a 10-year long U.S. program for exploring Mars. The program is designed to send pairs of inexpensive spacecraft to Mars every 26 months through 2005. By that time, NASA will have a fleet of small spacecraft with highly focused science goals probing and watching the planet, setting in place a new way of exploring the solar system. The objective is to conduct faster, better, and cheaper missions. Combinations of orbiters and landers will use the new microtechnologies of lasers, microprocessors and electronic circuits, computers and cameras the size of a one-inch cube, to deliver a wide array of miniaturized payloads to Earth's planetary neighbor, Mars.

Mars Missions 1998–2005

1998 (Combined cost $187 million, $26 million for microprobes)

- *Mars Surveyor '98 Orbiter* will study Martian atmosphere, including analyzing its water content during seasonal cycles.
- *Mars Surveyor '98 Lander* will assess past and present water reservoirs on Mars, as well as conduct chemical, topology, and mineralogy investigations and weather studies. It will also deliver two unique soil microprobes that can penetrate beneath the surface to analyze mineral specimens.

2001 (combined cost, approximately $200 million)

- *Mars Surveyor '01 Orbiter* is intended to learn more about the minerals and chemistry of Martian surface, including identification of surface water reservoirs.
- *Mars Surveyor '01 Lander* may be used to deliver a Russian rover or small station launched by a Russian launch vehicle. The alternative would be a U.S. rover for studies of chemistry and mineralogy.

2003 (Approximate cost $200 million)

- NASA is exploring the possibility of a rover that would be used for sample collection and catching for later pickup by a sample return mission.

2005 (Approximate cost $200 million)

- NASA is considering a Mars sample return mission if found to be affordable.
- International collaboration on all Mars missions will be important for exploring in the next decade. Many space agencies around the world are considering participation in the planning stages of future missions, including Russia, Japan, and European countries. Scientists from the United States are consulting with international partners regarding the best ways to combine their efforts in Mars exploration. This may result in new proposals for cooperative missions in the first decade of the 21st century.

#2381 Exploring Mars — 70 — *© Teacher Created Materials, Inc.*

The Martians Have Landed!

Off to Mars *(cont.)*

Build an Earth-to-Space-Station Shuttle

The Job:

Your team of engineers is to design a shuttle that will carry a crew of six astronauts to a space station in orbit 220 miles (407 kilometers) above the Earth.

What you need to do:

- Look at pictures of other shuttles like the *Space Shuttle* or the Russian *Soyuz* that take people from Earth to the *Mir* space station. Get ideas for your shuttle.
- Talk to the group designing the Space Station since your shuttle will have to link up to it to unload passengers carried from Earth. You will need to be sure there is a way to do this at the space station.
- Make drawings of several different types of shuttles that might work and select one of them.
- Think of ways to simulate a launch of the shuttle and test them. Some ideas might be these:

    balloon power using string, straw, and a lightweight shuttle taped to the balloon

    sling shot using a large rubber band to send it into space

    using vinegar and baking soda as fuel to launch the shuttle

- Build a scale model of the shuttle and find the best method to launch it.

What the shuttle must be able to do:

- Carry six astronauts and a crew of a pilot, first officer, and flight attendant
- Launch from Cape Canaveral, Florida, from one of the rocket sites or the runway
- Make the trip to the orbiting space station in three to four hours
- Reach a speed of 17,500 miles per hour (280,000 kph) to put it in the space station's orbit
- Link up to the space station and discharge the six passengers and return to Earth

Materials you might need for constructing the model shuttle:

- cardboard tubes (paper towel or toilet paper rolls)
- aluminum foil
- pieces of Styrofoam
- balsa wood
- stiff paper
- string, straws, balloons
- vinegar, baking soda, plastic soda bottle

Completing the project:

Write a description of your shuttle, giving details about how it will be launched from Earth and link up to the space station. Make pictures to show the step-by-step flight plan.

© *Teacher Created Materials, Inc.*   *71*   *#2381 Exploring Mars*

The Martians Have Landed!

Off to Mars *(cont.)*

Build an Earth-Orbiting Space Station

The Job:

Your team of scientists has been hired to design a space station which will orbit 220 miles (407 kilometers) above the Earth.

What you need to do:

- Look for pictures of space stations such as *Mir* and *Skylab,* as well as designs for those which may be built in the future. This will give you ideas for what your space station may look like.
- Find out what the living conditions would be like in space to help you know what will be needed in the space station to keep people alive.
- Make drawings of several different types of space stations and then choose which one is best.
- Talk with the group designing the shuttle that will bring people from Earth to be sure you include a docking area.
- Talk with the group designing the Mars transporter that will carry passengers off to Mars. You will need to have a docking port for that spacecraft also. It should not be in the same location as the shuttle docking area.
- Build a scale model of the space station. Make it so that it can be opened up to show the inside areas used for living quarters, greenhouses and farms, observation spots, and communication centers.

What the space station must be able to do:

- House up to 50 people. Half of these will live on board, while up to 25 others will be waiting for transports to return to Earth or go to the moon or Mars.
- Supply permanent living quarters for 25 people.
- Have hotel-like rooms for 25 people to stay a few days.
- Provide places to grow, prepare, and serve food.
- Have science laboratories for experiments, emergency health room, and recreation and entertainment centers.
- Have communication area so people can talk to their families, as well as to a command center back on Earth.

Materials you might need for constructing the space station model:

- cardboard tubes and circular pieces (pizza cardboards)
- aluminum foil
- pieces of Styrofoam
- shoe boxes
- fabric
- construction paper

Completing the project:

Write a description of your space station, giving details about how people will be able to come and go from it and stay on board for long or short periods of time. Make pictures to show the different parts of the space station.

#2381 Exploring Mars　　　　72　　　　*© Teacher Created Materials, Inc.*

The Martians Have Landed!

Off to Mars *(cont.)*

Build a Space-Station-to-Mars Transporter

The Job:

Your team of engineers has been hired to design transportation to carry passengers from the Earth-orbiting space station to Mars. This trip will take eight months.

What you need to do:

- Gather pictures from books and Web sites (NASA) to get ideas for your transporter.
- Find out what the living conditions would be like in space to help you know what will be needed in the transporter to keep people alive for an 8–10 month journey.
- Make several drawings of possible transporters and then pick the best one.
- Speak with the group designing the Space Station and those building the Mars Shuttle to find out what type of docking port the transporter will need to link up with them.
- Build a scale model of the transporter.
- Draw a map of the route it will take from Earth to Mars.
- Read information about future space transports to carry humans.

What the Mars Transporter must be able to do:

- House a crew of three plus six passengers. This will include all the food, air, and water they will need during the 8–10 month trip.
- Provide for waste management and safety, as well as communication with Earth and recreation during the journey.
- Remain in orbit around Mars as crew and passengers are transported down to Mars.
- Provide for life support systems such as food, water, air, waste management.
- Provide for private living areas.
- Provide for recreation needs such as exercise equipment and communication to and from home.

Materials you might need for constructing the Mars Transporter:

- cardboard tubes
- aluminum foil
- pieces of Styrofoam
- shoe boxes

Completing the project:

Write a description of your Mars Transporter, giving details about how people will be picked up at the Space Station, taken on the long journey to Mars, and then transferred to the Mars Shuttle for the trip down to the planet. Make pictures to show the step-by-step process for all of this.

© *Teacher Created Materials, Inc.*   73   *#2381 Exploring Mars*

The Martians Have Landed!

Off to Mars *(cont.)*

Build a Mars Shuttle

The Job:

Your team of engineers has been hired to design a shuttle that will transfer up to nine passengers between the surface of Mars and a Mars Transporter that ferries people between Earth and Mars. The Mars Transporter will orbit Mars during the exchange of passengers to and from the shuttle.

What you need to do:

- Look at pictures of other shuttles like the *Space Shuttle* and the Russian *Soyuz* that take people from Earth to the *Mir* space station. Get ideas for your shuttle.

- Talk to the group designing the Mars Transporter since your shuttle will have to link up to it to unload and load passengers. You will need to design a way to do this.

- Make drawings of several different types of shuttles that might work and select one of them.

- Design various methods of landing the shuttle on Mars and choose one of them.

- Talk with the group designing the Mars base to have them leave room for the landing site the shuttle will need.

- Make drawings of the landing site that will be used by the shuttle on Mars.

- Build a scale model of the shuttle and the landing site to add to the model of the base.

What the Mars Shuttle must be able to do:

- Transfer a total of nine passengers to Mars' surface. They do not all have to go at one time. Shuttles may be designed to carry small groups and make more than one trip to the transporter.

- Withstand heat of reentry through the atmosphere.

- Provide for human needs such as protection during landing.

- Land safely near the base on Mars.

Materials you might need for constructing the Mars Shuttle:

- cardboard tubes

- aluminum foil

- plastic containers with lids

- cloth for parachutes

Completing the project:

Write a description of your Mars Shuttle, giving details about how people will be carried between Mars and the Mars Transporter. Make pictures to show the step-by-step process for all of this.

#2381 Exploring Mars   74   © *Teacher Created Materials, Inc.*

The Martians Have Landed!

Off to Mars *(cont.)*

Build a Base on Mars

The Job:

Your team consists of scientists, engineers, and others who must design and construct a scale model of the first base on Mars for up to 50 people.

What you need to do:

- Ask your teacher to get the November 1988 issue of *National Geographic* with the article "Mission to Mars" which describes a base on Mars in 2050.
- Talk to the group designing the Mars Shuttle to find out what area they will need for their landing site.
- Make drawings of several different types of buildings which will be needed. These should be living areas for up to 50 people, including permanent and temporary members of the base. Include science laboratories, an observatory, a greenhouse to grow food, and a recreation area.
- Design spacesuits to be used when people leave the buildings. Make a sample spacesuit for a doll, or out of paper for a paper doll.
- Design and build a model of ground and air transportation for getting around Mars.
- Select the best location for the Mars base. Think about what you have learned about the weather on Mars. Place a marker on the Mars map to show where the base will be located.
- Design a way to bring water to the base from the polar ice caps or from underground.
- Decide on a name for this first base on Mars. Remember, this will be an international base.

What the base must be able to do:

- Provide living quarters for up to 50 adults, both permanent and temporary.
- Protect humans from dangers such as overexposure to sunlight, lack of oxygen, extreme temperatures, low pressure, and dust storms. This will be necessary inside and outside buildings.
- Have transportation for getting around Mars, such as long-winged gliders which can fly in thin Martian atmosphere and ground rovers.
- Have landing sites for shuttles which will take passengers between Mars and the transporters coming from Earth's space station.

Materials you might need for constructing the Mars Base model:

- plastic containers
- cardboard tubes and flat pieces
- construction materials such as Legos
- straws, string, tissue paper
- large sheet of foam board
- Styrofoam

Completing the project:

Write a description of the first Mars base, giving details about how people will be able to live and work there. Make pictures to show the inside of some of the scale model buildings.

© *Teacher Created Materials, Inc.*   *#2381 Exploring Mars*

The Martians Have Landed!

Postscript from Mars

The following is a summary of information released by NASA on August 8, 1997.

Landing on July 4, 1997, the Mars *Pathfinder* proved to be a huge success for NASA and JPL. This inexpensive lander and rover went well beyond fulfilling its goals of collecting data on Martian weather and minerals. Within the 30 days allotted for the initial mission, The *Sagan Memorial Station* and *Sojourner* Rover collected far more data on the atmosphere, weather, and geology of Mars than scientists had expected it could. Over 9,669 tantalizing pictures of the Martian landscape were relayed to Earth.

Everything went just as planned during the entry into the atmosphere, descent, and landing. The sequences happened on time, and the landing was within 13 miles of the target, after traveling 310 millions miles across space from Earth. Its initial descent speed was 140 miles per hour, only six miles faster than scientists had estimated. The 36-foot circular parachute slowed the descent, and the spacecraft hit the ground at 40 miles per hour. It bounced about 16 times across the landscape for about .6 of a mile before coming to a halt. It even landed on its base petal so its thumb-sized antenna could communicate the successful landing to a jubilant team on Earth.

Pathfinder's performance in the Martian atmosphere will be of great value to Mars *Global Surveyor,* which will aerobrake through it to circularize its orbit when it reaches Mars on September 11, 1997.

The rover did the first on-Mars analysis of rocks, finding a high silica content. This indicated more volcanic activity than scientists had thought possible on Mars. The weather information collected by the lander confirmed some conditions the *Viking* landers had 21 years ago. The meteorology mast on the lander has observed a rapid drop-off in temperatures just a few feet above the surface. One detailed 24-hour measurement set of temperatures changed 30-40 degrees Fahrenheit in a matter of minutes.

Sweeping color panoramas of Martian landscape by the imager on the lander at *Sagan Memorial Station* clearly show the surface of Mars has been changed by winds and flowing water.

Sojourner, a robust rover, captured the imagination of the public which followed the mission via the World Wide Web. There were 20 Web sites constructed by JPL with a record 565 million hits worldwide from July 1 to August 4. The highest volume of hits in one day was on July 8 with 47 million logged. The rover's performance surpassed its designers' minimum expectations. Built to last a week, the rover was still healthy after 30 days of roaming. It traveled 171 feet around the lander, taking 384 spectacular views of rocks and the lander. The wheels of the rover gave new information about the composition of Martian soil, as well as rocks around the landing site. It has endured extremely cold conditions, proving it was designed just right for Mars.

Data from the surface of Mars will continue to be collected and transmitted to Earth to be analyzed by scientists, as *Pathfinder* enters its extended mission period.

"The Martians will be us."

—Dr. Carl Sagan, *Cosmos*

Resources

Related Books and Periodicals

1996 Mars Mission NASA Press Kit, released November 1996. Order from JPL (see page 78). This 59-page booklet contains information about Mars, the history of Martian exploration, including Mars *Pathfinder* and Mars *Global Surveyor*. Drawings illustrate the features of these spacecraft as well as their paths from Earth to Mars and landing sequences.

Begley, Sharon. "Greetings from Mars: Special Report." *Newsweek,* July 4, 1997. This article provides excellent information, photographs, and drawings about the Mars *Pathfinder* mission.

Cole, Joanna. *The Magic School Bus® Lost in the Solar System.* Scholastic, Inc., 1990. This delightful book takes children on a unique field trip through the solar system aboard the Magic School Bus®. They travel past each of nine planets and the asteroid belt.

Collins, Michael. "Mission to Mars." *National Geographic,* November 1988. This outstanding article, written by the astronaut who piloted the command module on the *Apollo 11* mission, describes a future mission to Mars. The article includes drawings and photographs of the mission, astronaut training, the spaceship and route, and Mars Base 2050. This back issue (and others) are available by contacting National Geographic (800) 335-2624.

Final Frontier: Space Science Astronomy, August 1997 issue. This is a Mars special issue containing a variety of articles regarding Mars *Pathfinder.* An article on future human exploration of Mars is included.

Gallant, Roy A. *Our Universe.* National Geographic, 1994. (800) 447-0647. This outstanding picture atlas includes chapters for each of the planets, illustrated with NASA photographs and excellent information, as well as deep space objects, shuttles, and future space exploration.

Kluger, Jeffrey. "Uncovering the Secrets of Mars," *Time,* July 14, 1997. Outstanding text, photos, and diagrams depicting the launch and landing of the Mars *Pathfinder.* The colored photos on the cover and within the article, are 3-D images of the *Sojourner* and landing site.

Sagan, Carl. *Cosmos.* Random House, Inc., NY, 1980. Based on the 13-part television series by the same title, this book is the lay person's guide to astronomy. An excellent chapter on Mars includes history of the planet, as well as man's exploration through *Viking 1* and 2.

Young, Greg. *Exploring Mars: Challenging.* (TCM 2383) Teacher Created Materials, Inc., 1997. (800) 662-4321. This teacher's guide includes hands-on activities related to the Mars *Pathfinder* and Mars *Global Surveyor* missions (for students in grades 5–7).

Young, Ruth M. *Science/Literature Unit: The Magic School Bus® Lost in the Solar System.* (TCM 2086) Teacher Created Materials, Inc., 1996. (800) 662-4321. This teacher's guide contains a variety of hands-on activities to teach astronomy concepts, including a script for a simulation flight to a station on the moon.

Young, Ruth M. *Science Simulations: Challenging.* (TCA2107) Teacher Created Materials, Inc., 1997. (800) 662-4321. Simulations include a trip to Mars in the year 2025, as well as communicating with intelligent life beyond our solar system.

Resources

Related Materials

Astronomical Society of the Pacific (ASP). 390 Ashton Ave., San Francisco, CA 94112, (800) 335-2624. Request a free catalog showing a wide selection of materials related to astronomy, including slides, posters, videos, and computer software. Teachers are eligible for free copies of *The Universe in the Classroom,* a quarterly newsletter by ASP. Request this newsletter on school letterhead.

Edmund Scientific Co. 101 East Glouchester Pike, Barrington, NJ 08007-1380 (800) 728-6999. Carries colored filters, as well as variety of other hard-to-find science materials.

Jet Propulsion Laboratory (JPL), Mail stop CS-530, 4800 Oak Grove Drive, Pasadena, CA 91109. Video tapes and pictures on wide range of topics related to Mars exploration. The video *JPL Computer Graphics* (100 minutes) includes an animation of a flight over Mars, taken from the data gathered during the *Viking* missions. Excellent photographs, with information on the reverse side, are available on the Mars *Pathfinder* and Mars *Global Surveyor* missions. Video: *Mars Pathfinder* (limited supply). CD-ROMs: Mars *Navigator Interactive Multimedia,* describing *Pathfinder* and *Global Surveyor* missions (limited supply). Contact the Teacher Resource Center at JPL and request material on the Mars explorations. (818) 354-6111.

NASA's Central Operation of Resources for Educators (CORE), Lorain County JVS, 15181 Route 28 South, Oberlin, OH 44074 (216) 774-1051, Ext. 293. Provides material from NASA to use with students, including slides, videos, and photographs taken from satellites and space missions. Free catalog, request on school letterhead.

National Geographic Society, PO Box 2118, Washington, DC 20013-2118 (800) 447-0647. Supplies maps and posters such as The Heavens, The Earth's Moon, Solar System/Celestial Family, and The Universe. Back issues of *National Geographic* may be ordered. Call for catalog.

National Science Resource Center, Smithsonian Institution, MCR-502, Arts and Industries Bldg., Rm. 1201, Washington, DC 20560 (202) 357-2555. Order *Resources for Teaching Elementary School Science,* a comprehensive guide to science curriculum, teacher's references, ancillary resources, and lists of publishers and material suppliers.

National Science Teachers Association (NSTA). (800) 722-NSTA. Supplies books, poster, and CD-ROMs related to astronomy and other sciences. Order a free catalog of NSTA books and materials.

The Planetary Society, 65 North Catalina Ave., Pasadena, CA 91106-9899 (818) 793-5100. Order the 25 x 45 inch map of *Mars—An Explorer's Guide to Mars.* This map shows details of the planet, as well as pictures of details discovered during exploration by *Viking 1* and *2.* Request a catalog of other materials.

Sky Publishing Corp. P.O. Box 9111, Belmont, MA 02178-9111 (800) 253-0245. Offers variety of astronomical materials, including *Mars Map,* 39 x 40 inches, showing thousands of craters, mountains, and surface features mapped by *Mariner 9*, many of which are labeled.

United States Geologic Survey, Box 25286, Federal Center, Bldg. 810, Denver, CO 80225. (800) 435-7627. Offers a wide variety of maps of Mars, including Olympus Mons to Ares Vallis, Eastern Valles Marineris to Ares Vallis, Olympus Mons, Central Valles Marineris, and Area Vallis (*Pathfinder* landing site). Each map is about $4.00 and has a 3–4 week turnaround time.

Resources

Web Sites

Astronomy Cafe http://www2.ari.net/home/odenwald/cafe.html

Sten Odenwald, NASA-Goddard scientist, has listed 3,001 questions he answered about astronomical things. You can ask him questions as well. This is also a public information site for NASA's Image spacecraft, including science activities for educators and images of the space environment of Earth and sun-Earth interactions.

Center for Mars Exploration http://cmex-www.arc.nasa.gov/

NASA's Ames Research Center presents one of the best maintained Mars Web sites. Award-winning home page provides more than 65 links to Mars-related information divided into 15 categories. Check here for latest information about *Pathfinder* and *Global Surveyor.* Includes press releases, backgrounds, and many image links for complete in-depth coverage of Mars-related activities.

The Daily Martian Weather Report http://nova.stanford.edu/projects/mgs/dmwr.html

The Mars *Global Surveyor* Radio Science Team's outreach program will share data about the Martian atmosphere with students and teachers, shortly after it's collected from the spacecraft. Learn when and how Martian weather data will be collected and check *Surveyor's* current flight status report from JPL.

Imaging Mars http://barsoon.msss.com/http/new-directories/newhome.html

Malin Space Science designs, develops, and operates instruments that fly on unmanned spacecraft. It provides the imaging cameras for Mars *Global Surveyor* Orbiter and Lander. This site gives you a close-up look at the techniques for imaging Mars. Included here is a Mars *Global Surveyor* timetable.

MarsNet http://astrosun.tn.cornell.edu/marsnet/mnhome.html

This site links the amateur and the professional Mars-observing communities and showcases images from both. Come here for help planning your own Mars observations and learn how to submit your images to the MarsWatch Project. You can subscribe to the free *International Mars Watch Electronic Newsletter.* Finally, take a moment to input current data to see what Mars will look like from your location on Earth on the "Take a Look" page.

Mars Exploration Program http://www.jpl.nasa.gov/mars/

The Jet Propulsion Laboratory (JPL) offers comprehensive information about Mars projects and related points. Four main ideas of exploration provide details on different aspects of Mars missions. Great resources are on Mars Exploration Education page. The *Sojourner* page received "The Cool Robot of the Week" award.

Mars Pathfinder Cutouts http://mpfwww.jpl.nasa.gov/mpfwwwimages/education/lander-cutout-smal.gif

This site has three models which can be copied for students to cut out and paste together to form 3-D models of the Mars *Pathfinder* cruise stage, heat shield, and lander.

National Space Science Data Center http://nssdc.gsfc.nasa.gov/planetary

This is NASA's archive for lunar and planetary data and images. You can find out about past missions to the moon, Mars, and other planets, as well as chronology of lunar and planetary exploration.

© *Teacher Created Materials, Inc.*   79   *#2381 Exploring Mars*

Resources

Web Sites *(cont.)*

Additional Web Sites

- Arizona Mars K–12 Education Program: http://esther.la.asu.edu/asu-tes/
- Basic Mars page with links to other sites about Mars and its exploration: http://bang.lanl.gov/solarsys/mars.html
- Hot Wheels Web Site for more info about *Pathfinder* rover: www.hotwheels.com
- Mars *Global Surveyor*: http//mgs-www.jpl.nasa.gov
- Mars *Pathfinder*: http://mphwww.jpl.nasa.gov
- Mars *Global Surveyor* mission homepage: http://mgs-www.jpl.nasa.gov
- *Sojourner* rover information: http://mpfwww.jpl.nasa.gov/rover/descrip.html
- Weather on Mars: http://mpfwww.jpl.nasa.gov/ops/asimet.html
- 3-D printout of *Sojourner* microrover: http://www.lpl/arizona.edu/imp

CD-ROMs

Eyewitness Encyclopedia of Space and the Universe, DK Multimedia, New York, NY. (800) 356-6575. World Wide Web: http://www.dk.com. (Also available from ASP, listed under Related Materials.) Visually exiting learning adventure into outerspace aboard Skylab for a day, 3-D model of the space station *Mir.* Learn how it feels to live in space. Recommended for ages seven and up. System requirements: 2x CD-ROM drive, Mac:LCIII=, 8 MG RAM, System 7.0+, 256 color monitor; PC: 486/33+, 8 MG RAM, Windows 3.1+, sound card.

Mars Navigator, California Institute of Technology and Georgia Institute of Technology. Contact Catherine L. Davis: catherine.1.davi.jpl.nasa.gov. This disk contains animations and narrations about the Mars *Pathfinder* and Mars *Global Surveyor* missions. Included are six interactive experiences to help understand such topics as the motion of the moons around Mars and mission design. Compatible with Windows 3.1 and 95, as well as Macintosh.

NASA Ames Space Science Division, The Center for Mars Exploration, Mail Stop 245-1, NASA Ames, Moffett Field, CA 94035-1000. (415) 604-4217 http://cmex-www.arc.nasa.gov Request CD-ROM: The *Mars Educational Multimedia* which provides a Mars atlas, Mars-based lesson plans, descriptive information about Mars, image-processing software to get information from the images in the Mars atlas and from new images acquired by future orbiter and lander missions.

Views of the Solar System, National Science Teachers Association, Arlington, VA (800) 722-NSTA. A fantastic resource for everyone from young students to serious space enthusiasts. It is laid out like an Internet Web page with hypertext links and comes with Microsoft Internet Explorer. Information about sun, moon, planets, asteroids, comets, and meteors. Detailed views of the solar system. Click on Jupiter, for example, and you get information about each of the giant planet's 16 moons and the impact of fragments of comet Shoemaker-Levy 9. It even includes a recipe for making a model comet nucleus with dry ice and a few other simple ingredients. Compatible with both Windows 3.1 with DOS 6.0 or Windows 95 or Macintosh-68030 processor or faster, System 7.0 or higher.

#2381 Exploring Mars   80   *© Teacher Created Materials, Inc.*